Blood
on Coal

By the same author:

Warren James and the Dean Forest Riots

The Industrial Teagues and the Forest of Dean

Around the Forest

Four Personalities from the Forest of Dean

Man of Iron – Man of Steel
(The Lives of David and Robert Mushet)

The Story of Parkend (2nd edition)

The Diary of a Working Man
(edited by Ralph and Bess Anstis)

Fiction

Dean Forest Stories

Blood on Coal

The
1926
GENERAL STRIKE
and
MINERS' LOCKOUT
in the
FOREST OF DEAN

*'I don't believe God meant for a man to grovel in the bowels of the earth
and to leave blood on coal.'*
Jesse Hodges, Forest miner

Ralph Anstis

Black Dwarf
Publications

Underground at Lightmoor Colliery in the 1930s. Facing the camera and holding a carbide lamp is Bert Bowdler, whilst behind him, his 'butty' is undercutting the seam by hand – these were the days before machine working was introduced. The working conditions depicted here were typical of Dean mines, the seams generally being very shallow, about 2 – 3 feet.

~ CONTENTS ~

British Library Cataloguing-in-Publication Data. A catalogue
record for this book is available from the British Library

ISBN 0 9533028 4 9

Black Dwarf Publications
47 – 49 High Street, Lydney, Gloucestershire GL15 5DD

Image reproduction by Artytype,
5 The Marina, Harbour Road, Lydney, Gloucestershire GL15 4ET
Printed by Alden Press, Oxford

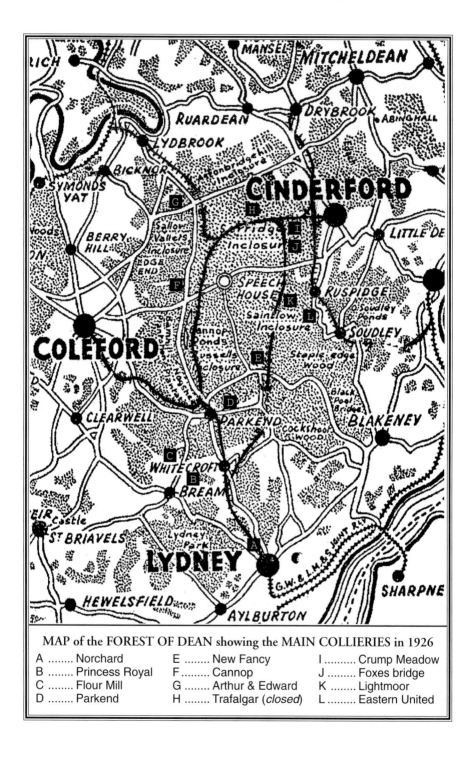

MAP of the FOREST OF DEAN showing the MAIN COLLIERIES in 1926

A .... Norchard	E .... New Fancy	I .... Crump Meadow
B .... Princess Royal	F .... Cannop	J .... Foxes bridge
C .... Flour Mill	G .... Arthur & Edward	K .... Lightmoor
D .... Parkend	H .... Trafalgar (*closed*)	L .... Eastern United

LIST OF ILLUSTRATIONS

Cont. over

Forest of Dean Miners' Association token
Lodge No, 10

PREFACE

There may well have been coal miners in the Forest of Dean when the Roman legions planted their standards on its hill tops and subdued the people who lived there. If so, they must have been few in number, though we know that Foresters were soon digging it for their Roman masters to burn in their fireplaces. By 1787 the numbers had increased, for the scratchy records of the times tell us there were 530 miners – men, women and children – working in about 106 small coal mines in the Forest. By this time the industrial revolution was advancing across Britain and was about to reach Dean. The rich seams of coal there became a valuable commercial commodity and attracted businessmen, bent on making their fortunes, from all over Britain. They arrived with expertise and guile. They shouldered aside the native pit owners with their primitive methods and economics, and introduced big business procedures. They invested in deeper pits served by expensive equipment and installed a more rigid master-servant relationship with their employees.

The country, eager to satisfy its industrial needs, demanded more and more coal, and more and more colliers to dig it. By 1871 the number of coal miners in Dean had increased to 2,900. Fifty years later it was 7,800. The Foresters never took kindly to the arrival of the 'foreign' intruders who exploited them and trampled on their old way of life, and they fought them at every turn.

This book tells part of the story of their struggle, how they fought them in 1926. John Williams, the union miners' agent in Dean at the time of the lockout in that year, said that a book about the struggle of his men would be 'a grim record of heroism and self-sacrifice'. Unfortunately, he did not write it and up to now it has remained unwritten. Until someone writes a better account, I offer this one. I dedicate it to the memory of the colliers of Dean and their families who suffered in 1926.

Ralph Anstis
Albion House, Coalway
Forest of Dean
October 1999

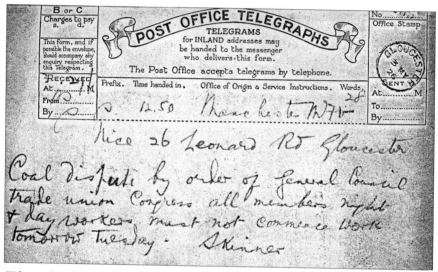

Telegraph ordering Gloucester transport workers to come out on strike in support of the miners, as from Tuesday 4 May 1926. This was the so-called Triple Alliance of miners, railwaymen and transport workers, striking in support of each other.

PRELUDE

- 1 -

The story of the lockout in 1926 and the General Strike it occasioned has its roots before the first World War; but we will start with the war. In 1914 the coal mines, which were the country's largest single industry, were owned and controlled privately, and there was a workforce of about 1,100,000 miners. During the war the Government was forced to take control of the industry, it not being possible to leave decisions about the production and distribution of coal to a multiplicity of small owners competing with one other. By the end of the war the owners were left with nothing but day-to-day management.

The Government had made the industry successful and efficient, in contrast to its state before the war. The miners were better paid and had a higher morale than ever before. They favoured more than a continuation of state control; they wanted state ownership. And they also wanted an increase in wages because of inflation, which was rising steeply.

The miners were enrolled in a score of trade unions, some big, some, like the Forest of Dean Miners' Association, small. Together they formed the Miners' Federation of Great Britain, an affiliation of unions, not a strongly-knit centralised body. The aims of the Federation were to reduce hours of work, increase wages, improve working conditions and safety in the pits, obtain better Workmen's Compensation, have union MPs in Parliament and secure the nationalisation of their industry. The total number of miners in Britain in 1918 was about a million. The miners in the Forest of Dean at that time numbered 7,000.

The mine owners for their part were united in the Mining Association of Great Britain. The Government was anxious to return full control of the mines to them but wanted to avoid conflict with the men. They realised that if they did try to return control to the owners and there was a strike, they might not win, even if, as they contemplated, they used the armed forces in the pits; and if they lost they would be forced to nationalise the industry. So to give themselves breathing time, they took up an option so often used by governments and set up a Royal Commission under Mr Justice Sankey, charging it with looking into the running of the coal industry and especially to report whether it should remain under state control or be given back to the owners. The Government promised to accept whatever the Sankey Commission recommended.

The Commission reported in April 1919. It proposed by a small majority that underground miners should have a seven hour rather than an eight hour day and that the mines should be nationalised. But the Government had never wanted nationalisation and, deciding the majority was too small, turned down the recommendation. However, they accepted that miners should have a seven hour day and embodied the change in an Act of Parliament in 1919.

Negotiations between the miners, the mine owners and the Government now took place on pay and conditions. Fundamental to the discussion were the facts that the owners wanted a return to pre-war conditions and the miners wanted nationalisation. There was no agreement and a five-day strike involving all one million miners took place in 1920. In January 1921, to calm ugly tempers and to secure time to effect a settlement, the Government made the coal owners a grant of £7m a month to subsidise miners' wages.

The owners, realising the subsidy would not last for ever, put forward a formula for dividing the money derived from selling coal into expenses (which included wages) and profits. The Miners' Federation rejected it, considering the formula no more than an attempt to beat down miners' wages. In spite of the lack of agreement between the two sides, the Government passed the mines back to their owners at the end of March, 1921. On 1 April the owners, with their traditional response to economic difficulties, decided to return to the old system of district bargaining and cuts in wages. In most cases the cuts involved a reduction of already inadequate wages by half and the miners said they would not accept the new terms. The Government, anticipating trouble, recalled troops from Ireland and other stations abroad.

The Forest of Dean Miners' Association was led by its agent, the charismatic H.W. Booth. He was a persuasive speaker but his men needed no encouragement from him to join with their fellows in the rest of Britain and refuse to go to work on the terms laid down. Like the other employers

Right: Miners about to descend at Trafalgar Colliery, circa 1921. By this date the pit was in difficulties, working through the early 1920s at a substantial loss, and it closed in 1925. Pumping operations continued for a while but were not maintained during the strike of 1926 and the workings became flooded.

Cage about to descend Trafalgar Colliery.

The homely but cramped conditions the miner went home to. This circa 1930 photograph shows his work clothes drying in front of the kitchen fire; note the work boots on the chair. The dirt-encrusted man of the house would no doubt have scrubbed down in a galvanised tin bath in front of this same fire, topped up with kettles of hot water, after a day's work at the coal face.

The Co-operative store at Cinderford around 1930. The Forest Co-ops gave credit to miners during the 1921 lockout, as did many other shops, in the form of credit coupons issued by the Forest union. After the lockout ended, a financially exhausted union found itself lumbered with £27,000 worth of coupon debts.

in the country, the Forest of Dean owners imposed a lockout, and 7,000 men in Dean now had no employment. A few men continued to go to work but their mates had no quarter for them. They resolved that blacklegs should be expelled from the union and members should pledge themselves not to work with them after the current crisis was over.

The view of the ordinary man in the coal pit was expressed in *The Citizen* by a Forest miner of forty-five years experience. He pointed out that the proposed wage was only slightly higher than that paid in July 1914, yet the cost of living figure, according to Board of Trade figures, was 141% above what it was in 1914. He continued, *'Now, Sir, while there are many things I do not know (I am like the blind man in the Scriptures) I know one thing – that the minimum wage of a coal hewer up to 31 March was 15s 3d* [a shift](the equivalent of £20 in 1999 – see Appendix 1). *If we had started work on 1 April the maximum wage would have been 8s 8d or 6s 6d* [after] *reductions. These are absolute facts. Then if we work three days a week, which we have been working since January, the most we are promised for a considerable time to come, would produce 26s less 1s 9d stoppages for Union, unemployment, and insurance, which would leave 24s 3d* (about £31 in 1999) *to keep the home going. These facts, known to every collier in the Forest of Dean, have stiffened his back for this struggle. We have not entered upon the struggle without counting*

15

the cost; we know all about the depleted funds of our Union caused largely through unemployment, and we realise what it will mean to our families; but better die of starvation in God's beautiful sunshine than to go back to servile labour and semi-starvation caused by a wage that is not sufficient to keep a man, to say nothing about a family and a respectable home.'

The *Gloucester Journal* was unsympathetic to the miners. It blamed extremists among them, in its issue of 2 April 1921, for the troubles in the industry. It deplored the subsidy, which would cost the country nearly £60m by the end of August, and asked if, with all the unemployment in the country, it was fair to expect other workers to pay to keep miners wages high. There was at the time a widespread view that the miners were overpaid, with a wage of £1 a shift allegedly being fairly common in Britain during the war. Siegfried Sassoon was induced to write in response:

'Why should a miner earn £6 a week?
Leisure! They'd only spend it in a bar!
Standard of Life! You'll never teach them Greek,
Or make them more contented than they are!

'That's how my port-flushed friends discuss the Strike.
And that's the reason why I shout and splutter,
And the reason why I'd almost like
To see them hawking matches in the gutter.'

A mass rally of Forest miners was held on 1 April 1921 in the large meadow adjoining the Speech House. This was a favourite meeting place for Foresters. Many a rally of miners had been held there, and more would be held in the troubled years to come. H.W. Booth, the miners' agent, addressing the meeting in his powerful and persuasive way, said the miners were fighting not only the owners but also the Government, and that the Government were using the owners to help do their dirty work of bringing down the wages of all workers for them. The miners cheered him and showed their determination to continue to stay out.

Like other unions in the country, the Forest union refused to allow men into the pits to do maintenance work, especially to keep them drained of water. In doing so, it realised it had a major weapon in its hands. However, the Dean owners, realising the permanent damage lack of pumping would do to their pits, took what steps they could against flooding. Lightmoor, New Fancy, Foxes Bridge, Crump Meadow, and Eastern United, all with the aid of office staff, volunteers, friends and relatives managed to keep

Above: The redoubtable Hon. Charles Bathurst, Lord Bledisloe, stoking the boilers at Norchard colliery in 1921; he was one of the major shareholders. Left: His sons, pictured about to push some empty drams into the mine, were also volunteers to the cause.

the pumps working (for a contemporary account of the efforts made to keep the pumps working at Lightmoor see Appendix 2). At Norchard, Lord Bledisloe himself stoked the boilers which supplied steam for the pumps. *The Daily Herald* suggested that the practice he was getting might be useful for the time when his Lordship had to earn his living.

A notable exception was Cannop Colliery. It was the most up-to-date and one of the biggest mines in the Forest, and much money had been poured into it. Normally it took 36 pumpmen – truly a large number – to keep the water down to a tolerable level but they were necessary since, so it was believed, water from the River Wye found its way into the mine. All

These underground views at Lightmoor Colliery were taken in the 1930s by Mr. Clifford, Superintendent of the local Mines Rescue team. The conditions are fairly typical of the larger Forest pits and would have changed little since the turn of the century. The view **above** shows a pair of loaded drams at the top of the 'Jinny', about to be hauled out of the mine by the pit pony. The drams were of elm construction with steel bracing and each held about 30 cwt. The miners seen here are W. Blewitt on the left and W. Harris. The 'Jinny' was the roadway from the coal face and the drams were pulled up it by cable. The photograph **below** shows two men turning the 'Jinny wheel' which wound the cable. Behind them is the ventilation door.

Above: A day spent working on hands and knees in the dark and dirt of the coal face can only be imagined – but these men did it for a lifetime. In minimal headroom, miners Priddy and A. Matthews beaver away at the coal face with their picks. Note the wooden props, cut from Forest timber and hammered into place with wedges top and bottom.

Right: Bert Bowdler 'road ripping' with a pick, after powder shot had been fired at the 20 inch seam to loosen the coal.

Men signing on at Lightmoor Colliery pay office following the cessation of the 1921 strike. This pit was part of Henry Crawshay's empire in the Forest.

the workings had been flooded since the stoppage had begun and the situation had got so bad that it was feared it might never re-open.

On 6 April Lloyd George, the Prime Minister, offered the Government's good offices to bring the owners and the miners together and resume discussions but only if the pumpmen returned to work. The Federation would not agree to that condition, so the meeting did not take place.

When the Government passed the mines back to the owners the miners appealed to the railwaymen and transport workers for help. These three groups of workers had in 1913 formed the Triple Alliance, the aim of which was to give one another support during industrial conflict. But the miners found their expected allies, using various excuses, refused to come out on strike to help them. Whatever the validity of their excuses, to the miners and the world their defection was a sorry failure in trade union solidarity, and the day they refused help, 15 April 1921, was forever after known as Black Friday.

The workers of Lydney showed bitter resentment at the betrayal. At a

Left: Police and miners at Princess Royal Colliery during the 1921 national strike. These men were probably strike breakers and therefore required police protection when going to and from work. Percy Moore, Managing Director of the mine, is seated in the centre of the second row and distinguishable by his fancy socks!

Cannop Colliery circa 1930. Sunk between 1906 and 1910, Cannop was one of the most modern pits in the Forest but, being particularly prone to flooding, was much at risk during strikes. Note the large number of trees on the site; this was a deliberate attempt by the owners to soften and blend in the buildings of the colliery in this most beautiful part of the Forest – quite an enlightened policy for the time. Cannop Colliery closed in 1960.

meeting there C.T. Cramp, the industrial general secretary of the National Union of Railwaymen, attempted to explain why the Triple Alliance had not come out on strike in support of the miners, but irate speakers from the floor claimed that 98% of the Lydney Branch of the NUR and 100% of the dockers would have come out if they had been called.

The *Gloucester Journal* was pleased that the railwaymen and transport workers would not support the miners. Everyone, it maintained, agreed that the coal owners had offered the miners the highest possible wages consistent with the profitable running of their collieries, and advanced the view that the miners were not striking for higher wages but equal wages between pits, and the real issue was nationalisation. However, in spite of these strictures, it did concede that *'there has come a determined opposition to pre-war conditions which allowed capitalists to amass great wealth whilst leaving the workers only sufficient to keep body and soul together.'*

On 18 April 1921 the miners in the Forest attended a meeting at the Speech House. A big contingent from West Dean marched there behind the Pillowell Brass Band. H.W. Booth, addressing them, said that the Triple Alliance had been held up as a gateway through which the workers were to reach heaven, but now they were disillusioned; the Triple Alliance was as dead as a doornail. He warned the railwaymen that, though the miners had been attacked first, their turn would come and they must be on their guard. All the same, he asked his audience not to be downhearted. In the past the miners of Dean Forest had fought for months at a time against cuts of 10%. This time it was 50%, but they must not despair.

The Forest Union had already distributed some strike pay to their men and in the third week of April gave more – six shillings each to adult men, five shillings to youths and one shilling and sixpence to boys. This payment exhausted their funds, but they arranged with the Forest Co-operative Societies to give credit to their members and private shops were invited to do likewise. The credit coupons issued would be redeemed when times became normal.

Meanwhile in the House of Commons Lloyd George said that the last thing the Government wanted was to see the miners starved into submission; he pointed out, however, that there were classes of the community whose standards of living had been reduced far more than the miners. The suffering among the professional and middle classes generally had been more than the public realised.

In July, in the eleventh week of the struggle, when belts in the Forest were being tightened even more than in the professional and middle classes, H.W. Booth, the miners' agent, announced that a new offer had been

PRINCESS ROYAL COLLIERY

PRICE LIST

HIGH DELF SEAM

STANDARD RATES - 1921

"Mercury" Office, Cinderford.

Princess Royal Colliery

PRICE LIST

HIGH DELF SEAM

Standard Rates, 1921

1. **Tonnage Rates.**
   Stret or Narrow Work. First working only 2/6
   Pillar Work 2/-

2. **Top Cutting and Bottom Lifting.**

6-ft. Centre Roads Inches	Rate	7-ft. Centre Roads Inches	Rate
6	8d.	6	1/4
7	9¼d.	7	1/5¼
8	10½d.	8	1/6½
9	1/-	9	1/8
10	1/1¼	10	1/9¼

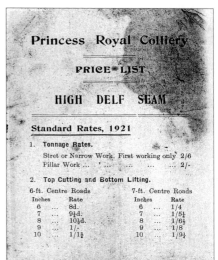

Rates of pay for miners working at Princess Royal in the early 1920s – other pits in the Forest would have been quoting broadly similar rates. As can be seen, it is quite detailed but for men working 'piece-work' rates, every extra inch of seam was important. The detail here also gives some indication of how difficult and involved any sort of negotiations with the miners were, and why they fought so hard to keep what they had. The list also covers work done by timbermen and trammers, and allows for rock cutting when coal was being searched for. Produced as a booklet issued to miners for their reference, pages 1 and 2 appear above, with 3 and 4 below, and 5 and 6 on page 25, right.

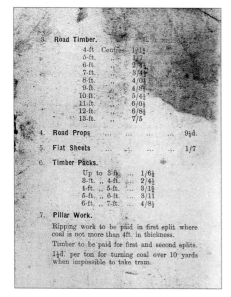

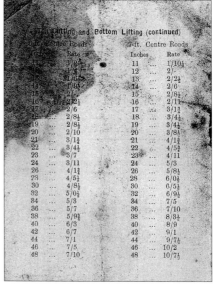

3. **Road Timber.**

4-ft	Centres	1/1¼
5-ft.	,,	1/7
6-ft.	,,	2/4½
7-ft.	,,	3/4½
8-ft.	,,	4/0½
9-ft.	,,	4/8½
10-ft.	,,	5/4½
11-ft.	,,	6/0½
12-ft.	,,	6/8½
13-ft.	,,	7/5

4. **Road Props** ... ... 9½d.

5. **Flat Sheets** 1/7

6. **Timber Packs.**

Up to 3-ft.	1/6½
3-ft. ,, 4-ft.	2/4½
4-ft. ,, 5-ft.	3/1¾
5-ft. ,, 6-ft.	3/11
6-ft. ,, 7-ft.	4/8½

7. **Pillar Work.**

Ripping work to be paid in first split where coal is not more than 4ft. in thickness.

Timber to be paid for first and second splits.

1½d. per ton for turning coal over 10 yards when impossible to take tram.

Top Cutting and Bottom Lifting (continued)

6-ft. Centre Roads Inches	Rate	7-ft. Centre Roads Inches	Rate
11	1/2½	11	1/10½
12	1/4	12	2/-
13	1/6½	13	2/2½
14	1/9¼	14	2/6
15	2/-	15	2/8½
16	2/2½	16	2/11
17	2/6	17	3/1¾
18	2/8½	18	3/4½
19	2/8½	19	3/4½
20	2/10	20	3/8½
21	3/1¾	21	4/1¾
22	3/4½	22	4/5¾
23	3/7	23	4/11
24	3/11	24	5/3
26	4/1¾	26	5/8½
28	4/5¼	28	6/0½
30	4/8½	30	6/5½
32	5/0½	32	6/9½
34	5/3	34	7/5
36	5/7	36	7/10
38	5/9¾	38	8/3½
40	6/3	40	8/9
42	6/7	42	9/1
44	7/1	44	9/7½
46	7/5	46	10/2
48	7/10	48	10/7½

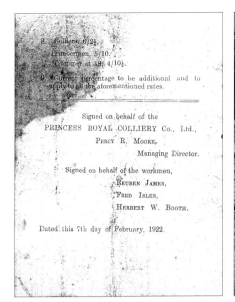

8. Colliers, 6/2½.
Timbermen, 5/10.
Hammer at 18, 4/10½.

9. Current percentage to be additional and to apply to all the aforementioned rates.

Signed on behalf of the
PRINCESS ROYAL COLLIERY Co., Ltd.,
PERCY R. MOORE,
Managing Director.

Signed on behalf of the workmen,
REUBEN JAMES,
FRED ISLES,
HERBERT W. BOOTH.

Dated this 7th day of February, 1922.

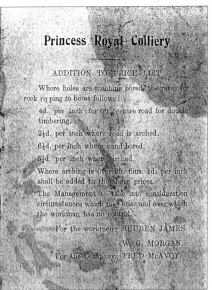

Princess Royal Colliery

ADDITION TO PRICE LIST

Where holes are machine bored, the rates for rock ripping to be as follows :

4d. per inch for 6ft. centre road for double timbering.

2½d. per inch where road is arched.

6½d. per inch where hand bored.

5½d. per inch where arched.

Where arching is over 2ft. 6ins. 1d. per inch shall be added to the above prices.

The Management to take into consideration circumstances which may arise and over which the workman has no control.

For the workmen : REUBEN JAMES.

W. G. MORGAN.

For the Company : FRED McAVOY.

received from the owners and the Federation had decided to ballot the membership on it. He was against the offer because it meant a great reduction in wages; and his men agreed with him and voted against accepting it with no hand raised in opposition. But nationally, wearying of the hardships imposed by the lockout, the miners accepted it by a large majority. The only areas supporting the Forest of Dean in their opposition were Bristol, Kent, Lancashire and Somerset – generally the smaller coalfields. As a result of the national decision the Federation Executive advised the men to go back to work on the owners' terms. Booth was despondent; he thought the way the men had been let down by their leaders was tragic. They had been out for 14 weeks and had nothing to show for it.

Thus ended the 1921 lockout. The Forest of Dean men went back to work disillusioned and resentful – and their union had the worry of the redemption of £27,000 worth of credit coupons.

- 2 -

The effect of the miners' defeat in July 1921 was to reduce coalmining to one of the worst paid jobs in the country. The average wage per shift went down to less than half of what it had been in the previous year when the mines had been under Government control. In Dean some colliers

Above: John Williams, miners' agent for the Forest of Dean and a member of the Miners' Federation of Great Britain national executive committee.

Right: Arthur J. Cook. He was Secretary of the MFGB from 1924 until his death in 1931, at the age of 46.

were working only one or two shifts a week and the minimum wage for an underground worker was 7s 9d a shift (the equivalent of about £10 in 1999), sometimes only 5s (about £6.50 in 1999) for a surface worker. The Miners' Federation tried to get improvements in wages to no avail. The owners replied that the way to more money was for miners to go back to a longer day.

In 1922 John Williams became the miners' agent in Dean. As he said when he assumed office, Dean was economically in the doldrums with poverty everywhere. He found the union had fewer than one-third of the miners in membership and that it was saddled with debt. Helped by his assistant, G.T.D. Jenkins, he set about strengthening the union. He was a man of drive and ability, and was soon elected to the Federation's national executive committee.

In 1924 there was a boom in export coal sales, and the Federation seized the opportunity to give notice that it wished to revise the wages agreement that had been forced on the men in 1921. A new Government had come into office at the beginning of 1924 – the first Labour Government – and the coal owners thought it wise to respond to the Federation's request for a revision of the agreement because of fear of what the new Government might insist on. They put forward suggestions for new wage rates. At first the miners refused to accept them but finally agreed to a new formula for wages, though they found it unsatisfactory.

In 1924 the miners found a great national leader in Arthur J. Cook. He was born the son of a soldier in 1885 in Somerset, but his family soon moved to South Wales. He went straight from school into the pit and worked underground for twenty-one years. In his early days he was a local preacher and the experience in the pulpit no doubt enabled him to hone his oratorial abilities to the excellent state for which he was renowned. For, as one colleague said, *'he talked like a Salvation Army preacher and swept over the industrial districts like a hurricane.'* He worked his way up the union hierarchy, between times going to the Central Labour College for two years, and became miners' agent in the Rhondda district. He was imprisoned in 1918 for strike activities and again in 1921 because of the part he played in the lockout in that year. After two spells on the executive of the Miners' Federation he was elected its secretary. But attaining this high office did not tame his spirit or restrain his exuberance. He came to be a mirror of the mood of the miners and they trusted him. His audiences were bigger even than those who came to hear Keir Hardie.

The year 1924 was a relatively prosperous year for Britain, including the mining industry, but in 1925 a steady decline in the country's economic state set in and the Chancellor of the Exchequer, Winston Churchill, put British currency back on the gold standard at the pre-war level. It would now be impossible to sell British goods abroad unless costs were cut, and the Prime Minister, Stanley Baldwin, said that the return to the gold standard meant *'all workers in this country have got to take reductions in wages.'*

A general attack on wages followed the Prime Minister's statement. It began in the coal industry, where the coal owners invited the miners to talk with them. The owners wanted a new agreement to replace the 1924 settlement. They proposed an average cut in wages of about $16\frac{1}{2}$ per cent, the abolition of the minimum wage and the abolition of the principle of national agreements. The last proposal would mean that wages would be settled between individual coal companies and their workers according to the economic ability of each district to pay, and would result in different rates in different coalfields. It now also became clear that the employers wanted to increase the seven hours spent each day at the coalface. Forest of Dean miners were especially concerned about the prospects for their wages because, except for Somerset miners, theirs were the lowest in Britain.

The national executive committee of the Miners' Federation of Great Britain, photographed at Scarborough in July 1925. Cook is seated in the centre of the second row, whilst Williams is the centre figure on the ground at the front.

Though the country's miners had not yet fully recovered from their big struggle of four years earlier, they refused to accept the proposals. John Williams, the Forest miners' agent, considered them a colossal insult, reducing miners to slavery and giving their employers the highest profits. Under the proposals miners would have to give up the principle of a minimum percentage added to their standard rates, which in the Forest would mean a reduction of about 15 per cent – at a time when they would need an *increase* to keep up with the cost of living. For a four day week, which Forest miners sometimes worked at this time, a surface worker with no percentage addition would be paid only 17s 6d (about £29 in 1999) a week. If he was unemployed and had a wife and three children his dole from the state would be 29s (about £47.50 in 1999).

In July the Forest Miners held their annual rally at the Speech House. The weather was fine; according to the *Dean Forest Mercury* the sun 'blazed forth with almost tropical ardour.'

FOREST OF DEAN MINERS' ASSOCIATION.

NOTICE.

MINERS' STRIKE.

STRIKE OR NO STRIKE

MASS MEETING

will be held at

SPEECH HOUSE

SUNDAY NEXT, AUG. 2nd, 1925, at 11 a.m.

Meeting to be addressed by

12534   **JOHN WILLIAMS, Agent.**

During the speeches, the Forest miners reiterated they would not accept starvation conditions and would fight to the bitter end for wages based on the cost of living.

There was similar vehement opposition to the owners' proposals throughout the country, but it had no effect on the coal owners. They gave the men notices discharging them with effect from 31st July. Collieries, the notices said, would be open for work on 1 August on terms which would be announced shortly. The colliery owners said they would not reduce the pay of men they wished to remain in post to maintain the pits during the dispute; and in the Forest the union agreed, as it did not in 1921, to allow men in the pits for this purpose provided the number was kept as small as possible.

Earlier the miners had appealed to the General Council of the TUC for help. The General Council had recognised the attack on the miners as a prelude to an attack on all workers, and promised to support them. They made it clear, as they were to reiterate many times later, that they were backing the miners' struggle to avoid a wage reduction and were not mounting political action against the Government. The railway and transport unions also pledged support. They agreed there should be a complete stoppage of all movements of coal if the owners implemented their proposals. The potentially powerful Triple Alliance was to operate at last.

Meanwhile discussions between the Prime Minister, the General Council and the Miners' Federation had begun. The Prime Minister was unflinching. He insisted that all workers had to face a reduction in wages to help put the country on its feet and that the mining industry must stand on its own economical basis; and he refused to give it a subsidy.

The General Council now played its trump card and announced there would be an embargo on moving coal from 1 August. The Government's reaction was immediate. Knowing they were unready for a direct conflict with the unions, they hurriedly convened a meeting with the coal owners and the miners and promised the owners a nine months' subsidy, the purpose of which was mainly to support wages. This humiliating change of policy was announced on Friday 31 July, which was subsequently known in Labour circles as Red Friday.

The Government also announced they would set up a Royal Commission under Sir Herbert Samuel to inquire into the industry and make recommendations for improving it. It was known as the Coal Commission. Unlike the Sankey Commission which consisted of 13 members, six of whom were acceptable to the miners, the Samuel Commission was to consist of only three members none of whom was to be a working-class representative. Cynics suggested that the real purpose of the subsidy and the Commission was to give the Government time to organise themselves so that they might smash both the miners and the General Council should they still be belligerent nine months later when the subsidy was due to end and the Commission due to report.

As a result of the Government's announcement of a subsidy and a Royal Commission, the TUC rescinded their orders for the embargo. The Government could not conceal the fact that they had yielded to the General Council and the Triple Alliance and had suffered a humiliating defeat. But another day would come.

Not all coal owners were against nationalisation provided it was worth their while. Thomas Hedges Deakin, who owned the Parkend pits and had large interests in South Wales, wrote in the *South Wales News* that as a small colliery owner he would welcome the state taking over his collieries and transferring their value into Gilt-edged securities bearing a fair percentage of interest.

His willingness for his mines to be nationalised is not surprising when one considers figures issued by the Mines Department of the Board of Trade at this time. They showed the bad state the Forest coal industry was in and how impossible it was for mine owners in the Forest of Dean with their current methods of operating to pay the old wages without a subsidy. Their costs in 1925 amounted to £276,600 and sales brought in only £247,800, a loss of £28,800. It was only with the Government subsidy of £49,290 that the miners' wages could be paid and the owners make a profit. This sad situation was partly because output per shift was bad due to faults in the seams, and also because of the cost of pumping: an unparalleled amount of water collected underground and was often pumped from one colliery to another. But explanations do not alter facts. The output per shift in the Dean coalfield was the lowest in the whole country. The poor financial state of Forest mines was, of course, the main reason why Forest miners did not want their wages calculated according to the economics in their own area but on a national basis.

Other Mines Department figures show that a total of £15m was paid nationally in subsidy to coal owners from August 1925 to the end of January 1926. Of this sum £100,000 had been paid to the Forest of Dean. The Mines Department pointed out that the subsidy had not gone to supplement wages but to make coal cheaper, thus increasing demand for it. Three months later the figure went up to £22m for the nation and £130,000 for the Forest.

In the meantime the Government organised their resources to fight the unions at the end of the nine months' respite they had given themselves. They encouraged mine owners and industrial concerns which used coal to pile up large reserves of it – at Lydney an enormous stock was accumulated by the West Gloucestershire Power Co. And they set up an elaborate organization in which Britain was divided into ten areas, each of which was under a Civil Commissioner, who in an emergency would give decisions on behalf of the Government. The Forest of Dean was put in the South West Division, whose Commissioner was the Rt. Hon. Earl Stanhope, DSO, MC. A body called the Organisation for the Maintenance of Supplies was also set up to register citizens who were prepared to give voluntary help to maintain food supplies and water, fuel and public services. It was in fact a strike-breaking organisation. All the machinery was ready by April 1926 and would move on receipt of one telegraphed word: '*Action*'.

On the trade union side no organisation was planned, either nationally or locally. By now the views of the General Council of the TUC had moved to the right and, though it reaffirmed its support for the miners, many of its members accepted that a fall in wages was inevitable. The Miners' Federation, noticing the General Council's cooling off, decided not to hand over their case to them unreservedly, but to entrust them with it subject to consultation with themselves. They tried later to get the Council to agree to adopt the essence of the slogan that Cook had devised, '*Not a penny off the pay, not a minute on the day*,' but were unsuccessful.

One view of Cook's slogan; an unimpressed British Bulldog listens to the miners' chant.

– 3 –

The Coal Commission reported on 6 March 1926. They recommended an immediate reduction in wages and the reorganisation of the industry at some unspecified date in the future. They rejected the idea of nationalisation of the industry and could see no reason to continue the subsidy. It was, they said, indefensible to tax people in other industries to provide profits for the coal owners or to subsidise the wages of their workers. Miners in some areas earned an average of 76s a week, while in unsubsidised industries, shipwrights earned 56s and enginering fitters 57s. The cost of production with present hours and wages were greater than the coal industry could bear and wages would have to come down, though by how much depended on the coalfield. The amount would be greatest where the gap between costs (including wages) and income was biggest.

The Commission reported that the Government subsidy in the Forest of Dean amounted to about 2s 3d per ton despite low wages and the barest of profit for the owners. In some of the Forest collieries visited by the Commission output was hindered by a shortage of tubs, bad roads, insufficient mechanical haulage and antiquated equipment. In the Forest, as elsewhere, they found excessive underground travelling on foot. This, they said, could be obviated by sinking additional shafts or by riding men in, though in some cases it was difficult, if not impossible, to do this because of varying inclinations and the tortuous nature of the underground roads, due to the way they had been initially built. The average distance from pit bottom to the workplace was just under a mile, slightly less than the average for Great Britain, but the time taken to cover it was twenty-four minutes, slightly longer than the average. The Commission did not remark on the fact that at Cannop 'ditties' (small trucks on a steam railway) were at that time carrying men to the coal face. The time taken to lower men down the shaft and bring them up again was also longer in Dean – 85 minutes. But in spite of their gloom, the Commission believed that *'because the Forest cannot guarantee a standard of living absolutely up to the minimum thought necessary in Yorkshire it does not follow that mining in the Forest of Dean should cease to exist.'*

The Government accepted the report in general. In some districts, where its acceptance would impose a heavy sacrifice, they said they would continue a subsidy temporarily, say for three months, to help reach a settlement. But it was clear that before the Forest received any of this new subsidy Forest miners would have to accept the principles of the report.

The owners also accepted much of the report, saying they would do all they could to increase the efficiency of the industry. However, they were determined that negotiations between themselves and the unions should be on a district basis, although they would agree centrally a broad national agreement as a basis for local agreements. They also advocated an eight-hour working day whereas the Commission had been content that it should remain at seven.

The reaction of the miners to the report was spontaneous: they rejected it. This was understandable when one bears in mind that in the previous month 300,000 out of 950,000 of them, up and down the country, had earned less than £2 (about £68 in 1999) a week. They said they would starve before they accepted any reduction in wages.

At the beginning of April the Federation hastily summoned a conference of representatives from their constituents to discuss the report. John Williams attended for the Forest. He argued that the continuation of current pay was not enough and berated the Executive for dropping the Federation's policy of pressing for an increase in wages. He moved conference should reject the Commission's report and formulate alternative proposals. He lost his motion but conference agreed at least to fight against a reduction in wages pending reorganisation of the industry.

On 13 April 1926 representatives of the coal owners and the Federation met. The Federation refused to discuss a national agreement if it did not provide for a uniform national minimum wage; the owners refused to discuss a national wage and would not at first disclose the new rates they had in mind. However, the Federation gathered that they proposed to lower wages considerably, reducing them to 4 per cent below the 1914 levels in some parts and above that level by up to 20 per cent in others. The severity of the cuts can be gauged from the fact that the cost of living

Lightmoor Colliery directors at a meeting in Gloucester in 1921.

index showed that prices were then more than 70 per cent above the 1914 level (see Appendix 1).

When the coal owners did disclose details of the new wage rates they proposed, they explained they had drawn them up on two bases, on a seven and on an eight hour day. The first, on a seven hour day, showed a big reduction on current rates; the second, based on an eight hour day, gave higher wages. A.J. Cook, the Federation Secretary, said that under these new rates even the lowest paid man, whose wages had been a scandal, would suffer a reduction.

No agreement was reached between the two sides, and it was clear that none was likely without the intervention of the Government. The Prime Minister was invited to intervene and he met the parties the following day. Though the Federation had not accepted the Commission's Report, they nevertheless asked the Government for more financial help. In the words of J.H. Thomas, a member of the TUC General Council, they *'begged and pleaded . . . almost grovelling.'* But the Government refused. It was now ready for confrontation.

The coal owners prepared to impose their wage cuts. On Friday, the last day of April 1926, the subsidy ended and on the same day lockout notices appeared at the pit-heads. In them the men were informed that their contracts would terminate that day but the pits would be open on the following day at reduced rates of pay. The new rates would mean that Dean men would suffer a reduction of $25^1/_2$ per cent in their wages. The owners said that with the disappearance of the Government's subsidy the new rates meant that they would be left with no profit at all.

On the following day, which was May Day, the General Council of the TUC asked a specially summoned conference of trade union executives for a mandate to call a general strike in support of the miners. It was to begin at midnight on Monday 3 May. The voting figures were:

FOR A STRIKE 3,653,529
AGAINST 49,911
AWAITING INSTRUCTIONS 319,000

The news of the result of the ballot was received with joy by the miners in the country and by their fellow workers, though some trade union activists were suspicious when they learnt that J.H. Thomas and Ramsay MacDon ald were to be spokesmen for the strike. Two more right-wing men than they could not be found in the Labour Party, they said. Thomas especially did not believe in a general strike. He said so in as many words in the first speech he made after the conflict had begun. Even so, the General Council said they would reach no settlement without the miners' agreement and began to organise the strike.

The Government professed concern at the thought of a general strike and held discussions with the General Council. But they made it clear that no solution could be found unless the Coal Commission's report was accepted by all parties. If it were, the reorganisation of the industry could be put in hand immediately and, pending the results, an adjustment of wages and hours could be reached that would allow the industry to carry on economically. But the Government would continue negotiations only if the threatened general strike, which involved a challenge to the constitutional rights and freedom of the nation, was withdrawn.

On the Sunday evening of 2 May the Home Secretary issued the following notice:–

ALTHOUGH DISCUSSIONS ARE STILL PROCEEDING, IN VIEW OF THE ACTION OF THE TUC THE COUNTRY MUST BE PREPARED FOR A GENERAL STRIKE IN MANY INDUSTRIES AND PUBLIC SERVICES ON MONDAY NIGHT. THE GOVERNMENT HAS TAKEN ALL STEPS TO MAINTAIN THE SUPPLY OF FOOD, FUEL, LIGHT AND POWER; THE PROTECTION OF ALL ENGAGED IN THESE SERVICES; AND FOR THE PRESERVATION OF LAW AND ORDER. RECRUITING STATIONS FOR VOLUNTEERS WILL BE OPENED TOMORROW. ALL LOYAL CITIZENS SHOULD HOLD THEMSELVES IN READINESS TO ASSIST THE GOVERNMENT. FULL INFORMATION WILL BE ISSUED TOMORROW, BUT IN THE EVENT OF ANY DIFFICULTY OCCURRING IN FINDING THE RIGHT OFFICE ON TUESDAY INQUIRIES SHOULD BE MADE AT THE NEAREST POLICE STATION.

On the same Sunday the General Council requested more negotiations with the Government. They said they believed that, even though it involved some reduction in wages, they had a solution that could form the basis of agreement. Later that evening, led by J.H. Thomas, they met Government representatives in a room in 10 Downing Street and tried to persuade them to agree to their compromise. While they were thus engaged the Prime Minister asked them to come to his room. *'Gentlemen,'* he said, *'I am sorry to say our efforts for peace are unavailing. Something has happened at the* Daily Mail *and the Cabinet has empowered me to hand you this letter.'*

The letter referred to an unauthorised lightning strike by machine men on the *Daily Mail* who had refused to print an exceptionally violent leading article attacking Labour which contained the following:

'A general strike is not an industrial dispute. It is a revolutionary movement, intended to inflict suffering upon the great mass of innocent persons in the community and thereby to put forcible constraint upon the Government. It is a movement which can only succeed by destroying the Government and subverting the rights and liberties of the people. This being the case, it cannot be tolerated by any civilised government, and it must be dealt with by every source at the disposal of the community. A state of emergency and national danger has been proclaimed to resist the attack. We call upon all law-abiding men and women to hold themselves at the service of King and Country.'

The letter asked the General Council for a repudiation of the *Daily Mail* workers' action and the withdrawal of the instructions for a general strike. J.H. Thomas immediately disowned the *Mail* workers' action and with the other General Council representatives withdrew to draft a reply to the Government's ultimatum. Having done so, they went downstairs to present it but found the Prime Minister's room empty and dark. It was now after 3.30 am. A servant informed them that everybody had gone to bed and they had better go home.

The Government had decided on war.

THE GENERAL STRIKE

- 1 -

The General Strike in 1926 was the most important industrial conflict in Britain's history. Never before or since have organised working people given their moral support to, worked for and given up their wages for any group of workers for so long a time.

The General Council of the TUC had drawn up a plan for calling out industries in sections. The first men came out on Tuesday 4 May, which was thus the first day of the strike. They were transport workers on sea, land and air; the whole printing trade; iron and steel workers, metal workers and chemical workers; building workers except those on hospital and housing works; and electrical and gas workers supplying power for industry. Sanitary services and health and food services were not interfered with. Some branches of the National Sailors' and Firemen's Union did not come

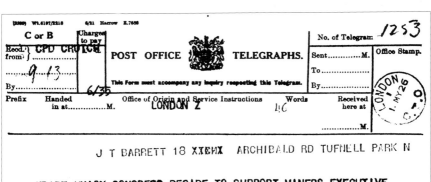

Telegram of 1 May 1926 telling London bus and tram drivers to stop work in support of the miners – the Triple Alliance at work.

out, but this was the only exception of importance in all Britain.

Tuesday 4 May heralded a different Britain. It began with an unknown stillness; there were no trains, no buses and no trams. Apart from a few blacklegs here and there, members of the unions obeyed the TUC's call 100 per cent. Many workers not called upon to strike came out as well – 32,000 textile workers in Paisley alone showed their support for the miners by striking. Even newly formed black-coated unions like the Railway Clerks' Association came out. Eighty two unions were wholly or partly on strike; altogether about two million people came out.

Support for the miners, though widespread, varied greatly from place to place. It was weakest in rural and middle-class districts and strongest in mining areas. In Gloucester, however, dockers, transport workers, railway men, engineers and printers came out, even though there was not a single colliery within a dozen miles of the city.

Many employers were not slow to react. For example a notice posted at Danks, Emlyn Ironworks in Gloucester stated:–

> **ANY MAN WHO ABSENTS HIMSELF WITHOUT OUR APPROVAL WILL BE CONSIDERED TO HAVE ENTIRELY LEFT OUR SERVICE. THIS IS NOT AN ORDINARY DISPUTE, BUT A TRIAL OF STRENGTH OF A HANDFUL OF COMMUNISTS AGAINST THE GOVERNMENT OF THIS COUNTRY.**

The enthusiasm of the rank and file at the business end of the strike was not reflected at TUC headquarters. Most of its General Council members were too old or uninspired to deal with the difficulties of running a general strike (or a national strike as they preferred to call it) and its negotiating committee gave no effective directions or advice to local strike committees. Many Council members dreaded the strike weapon they had chosen and wanted only to lay it down. The two mining members on the General Council absented themselves through the whole period. One was sick but not seriously, the other just went home and stayed there. Liaison between the TUC negotiating committee and the Federation was poor. The work at TUC headquarters fell on a small handful of men who were soon overworked and exhausted.

Individual trade unions provided what the General Council lacked. The headquarters of the unions sent instructions to their local branches on how the strike should be managed. Locally the unions were vitalised; non-members joined up, and lapsed members rejoined, encouraged by real

MESSAGE FROM THE PRIME MINISTER

Constitutional Government is being attacked. Let all good citizens whose livelihoood and labour have thus been put in peril bear with fortitude and patience the hardships with which they have been so suddenly confronted. Stand behind the Government, who are doing their part, confident that you will co-operate in the measures they have undertaken to preserve the liberties and privileges of the people of these islands. The laws of England are the people's birthright. The laws are in your keeping, you have made Parliament their guardian. **The General Strike is a challenge to Parliament and is the road to anarchy and ruin.**

STANLEY BALDWIN.

Guarantee to ALL Workers.

"It is not wages that are imperilled; it is the freedom of our very Constitution.

"**No man who remains at work shall be prejudicially affected afterwards.**"—Mr. Baldwin in the House of Commons, May 3rd, 1926.

EDWARD A. IND, PRINTER, 104, NORTHGATE, GLOUCESTER.

To Members of Trades Unions.

Work Stoppage by Trades Union Council.

Sir John SIMON, Attorney General under Mr. Asquith, said in the HOUSE of COMMONS, on Thursday, the 6th May, 1926:—

The decision of the Council of the **TRADES UNIONS** Executive to call out **EVERYBODY** regardless of the Contracts which these Workmen had made was not a lawful Act, and every Workman who had come out voluntarily or otherwise had broken the Law.

Every **MAN** who was out in disregard of his Contract was **PERSONALLY** liable to be sued in the County Court.

Every Trade Union Leader who had advised that course of action was liable in **DAMAGES** to the uttermost farthing of his **PERSONAL POSSESSIONS**.

Any Rule laying down that a **TRADE UNIONIST** forfeited his benefits if he did not obey the orders of his Executive meant that he would so forfeit those benefits if the order was lawful.

IT SHOULD BE PLAINLY KNOWN THAT THERE WAS NO COURT IN THIS COUNTRY THAT WOULD UPHOLD A RULE THAT A PERSON WOULD FORFEIT HIS BENEFITS IF HE WAS FORCED TO DO THAT WHICH WAS ILLEGAL.

TO ALL WORKERS IN ALL TRADES
OFFICIAL.

The BRITISH CONSTITUTIONAL GOVERNMENT state that effectual measures will be taken to prevent the Victimization by TRADE UNIONS of any Man who remains at work, either now or in the future, and no man will be left unprotected by the STATE from reprisals.

EDWARD A. IND, PRINTER, 104 NORTHGATE, GLOUCESTER.

action that was happening at last. Local strike committees and other organisations took on the job of organising strike business with gusto. Some of them, even in the nine days the strike lasted, became remarkably efficient; they ran sub-committees for food, workers' defence, intelligence, sports, communications, prisoners' aid, mass picketing and others. The strike had turned into a struggle with the Government, and local strike committees developed into organs of government themselves. Their efficiency and effectiveness in running the strike steadily increased up to the very end. Employers were more and more forced to come to strike headquarters as the real centres of authority, asking for permission to do certain things like moving food and coal. The hitherto cap-in-hand position between employer and employee was reversed.

Plans for the railways and other services made by the Government's strike organisation broke down the first day, and its Commissioners had to do the best they could either by negotiating with the strikers or introducing a scratch service with volunteer drivers. The TUC allowed food and certain other goods to pass; vehicles carrying them were brightly marked 'PERMIT FROM THE TUC' in black on yellow.

The Government called for volunteers to become police specials, and 40,000 applied in London and 200,000 in the provinces. They called out the troops in readiness and made an ostentatious display of power by ordering armoured cars to patrol the streets. There were some violent conflicts. On the second day there were confrontations between the police and strikers in Camden Town and Poplar in London involving baton charges by the police. On the fifth day there were riots in Glasgow, Hull and Middlesbrough, and baton charges in Newcastle and Preston, with many arrests.

On the eighth day there was an incident at Gloucester docks involving 300 to 500 pickets. Pickets succeeded in persuading the crews of two barges and a tug not to sail to Tewkesbury, so the owners announced they would use volunteer labour. These blacklegs were protected by a strong band of policemen, and scuffles broke out between pickets and police. The police won and the barges and tug set sail. The next day the owners, encouraged by their success, proposed to send a tug and an empty lighter along the canal to Sharpness with scab labour to pick up a cargo. Striking dockers tried to stop the tug from sailing by preventing the bridgeman from opening the swing bridge. Police were rushed to the scene. Hissing and booing, the crowd refused to give way and the police made a baton charge to force the pickets from the bridge. Eventually the tug and lighter got through. Fourteen men were arrested and thirteen of them were later sent to prison for fourteen days with hard labour. The other man was acquitted.

The Government was supported by the right-wing Economic League, which published news sheets and leaflets attacking 'the pernicious influence of the reds' and encouraged the enrolment of volunteers to drive trains, buses and lorries and carry out other strike-breaking activities. For some volunteer strike-breakers, for example undergraduates driving buses and trains, the strike was fun.

Because of strike action only 40 out of 1,870 newspapers in the country were published. The national dailies with extreme difficulty produced single sheets, many of which circulated only for a few miles round their offices. *The Times* was on two sides of a foolscap sheet but the *Western Mail* went to four pages and *The Spectator* to eight, though it was cyclostyled not printed. The Government, realising the need to give its viewpoint to the people, published from the *Morning Post* offices *The British Gazette*. It was edited by Winston Churchill. In its first issue he identified the conflict as being between trade union leaders and Parliament, and said the strike was revolutionary, indeed communist inspired.

The BBC was a dangerous enemy of the strikers. It was firmly under Government control and was not averse to broadcasting false news of large-scale returns to work. The trade unions cyclostyled and printed strike bulletins to counter this propaganda, and at first Labour Party headquarters telephoned corrections, but stopped doing so on finding that they were never used.

The TUC had its own official strike news bulletin, *The British Worker*, which was printed at the *Daily Herald* offices. It emphasised that the strike was an industrial dispute: '*No political issue has ever been mentioned or thought of in connection with the strike. It began over wages and conditions of working; it has never been concerned with anything else.*' In addition strike sheets giving local strike news were issued by some local trades councils. In Gloucester the sheet was called the *Gloucester Strike Bulletin*. It was issued with the permission of the local printing trade union branches and cost $1\frac{1}{2}$d. The first issue came out on Thursday 6 May, the 3rd day of the strike. Its editors were Edwin Bywater and Morgan Philips Price, who was later to become the Forest MP and to represent it for 24 years.

Right: The following six pages show examples of newspapers produced during the General Strike. The Daily Mirror *was cyclostyled rather than printed.* The British Gazette *was the Government's mouthpiece, whilst* The British Worker *put the viewpoint of the Trades Unions. The local paper the* Gloucester Strike Bulletin *was also produced by the Union side.*

Rupert

Daily Mirror

No. 2   NEWS BULLETIN.   One Penny
Thursday, May 6th, 1926.

London "CARRIES ON".

"Carrying On" described the situation on the second day of the Strike. Apart from a few minor incidents general calm prevailed throughout the country and the public cheerfully and helpfully shouldered the inconveniences which the strike brought in its train. Londoners were wonderful and the manner in which transport difficulties were overcome, despite midday gloom, was admirable.

ARRESTS IN POPLAR.

On Tuesday evening excitement ran high in Poplar and Canning Town. Three arrests were made at Poplar and two arrests at Bow.

When the crowd became aggressive a number of police baton charges were made. Numerous casualties occurred and the injured were taken to Poplar Hospital which is opposite Blackwall Tunnel. The injuries were mostly of a head character.

The Rioters' objective appeared to be the prevention of the passage of cars and one motor car was wrecked. Where drivers had no passengers the vehicles were allowed to proceed, but cars containing girls and others returning from work were stopped and passengers were forced to proceed on foot.

SIX 'BUSES ATTACKED.

Six 'buses were attacked and disabled by strikers at Hammersmith. One arrest was made.

STOCK EXCHANGE.

Stock Markets steady at lower level. War Loan $99\frac{3}{8}$. French Franc 153½.

WARSHIPS LANDING FOOD.

Two warships, H.M.S. Ramilies and H.M.S. Barham landed food supplies, mainly yeast, at Liverpool.

"THE BRITISH GAZETTE"

The first number of the Government's newspaper "The British Gazette" - four pages of seven columns, printed back and front - was published by His Majesty's Stationery Office, price one penny, for distribution by the Civil Commissioners whose districts cover the whole country.

It included a "Reply to strike-makers' plan to paralyse public opinion", which points out that silencing the Press would result in "rumours poisoning the air, raise panics and disorders, and carry us all to depths which no sane man would care to contemplate".

LIGHT AND POWER.

Members of the Electrical Trades Union in the London Power stations ceased work.

There is no likelihood of power or light being cut off in London. The Government have an adequate supply of volunteers to maintain services in the event of other Unions coming out.

OUR LEADING ARTICLE.

The people expect the Government not to fail in its duty. If the Cabinet surrenders, democratic government will be for ever impossible in this country. The nation is firm. It is calm and confident. There must be no provocation. Let us all pursue our daily tasks tranquilly, helping each other, offending nobody.

PRINTERS RETURN TO WORK.

Compositors, printers and stereotypers returned to work and the "Sheffield Telegraph" and "Sheffield Independent" published again at midnight. At Rugby the compositors including a labour official returned to work declaring that the strike was unconstitutional.

OFFICER DRIVES TRAIN.

When a train with troops and sailors leaving Portsmouth had left Pratton, the first station out, the driver left the engine. An officer on the train stepped into the cab, examined the levers and drove the train on.

STRIKE BREVITIES.

Mr. Baldwin presided over a full meeting of the Cabinet.

All news messages are from Reuters and other agencies.

Eight London Theatres have closed. Others may do so.

Deliveries of letters are being made in London daily at 9 a.m., 11 a.m., and 4 p.m.

There was a heavy supply of meat at Smithfield.

Worthing market gardeners pooled lorry resources to take produce to London.

PRINTED FOR AND PUBLISHED BY
DAILY MIRROR NEWSPAPERS LTD.
23-29, BOUVERIE STREET, LONDON, E.C.

43

DAILY EXPRESS

No. 8123.   SATURDAY, MAY 8, 1926.   ONE PENNY.

General Strike Illegal. Famous Lawyer's Opinion.

Light was thrown on the legal aspect of the strike by Sir John Simons, one of the foremost authorities on Industrial Law, speaking in the debate in the House of Commons on the Emergency Regulations.

"The General Strike," he said, "is not a Strike at all. A strike properly understood is perfectly lawful but the decision of the Trades Union Congress to call out everybody regardless of contracts and without notice is not a lawful action at all. Every workman who is bound by a contract to give notice before he leaves work and who in view of that decision has either chosen of his own free will or has felt compelled to come out without proper notice has broken the law, just as much as the coal owner would have broken the law if he had failed to give due notice to terminate the existing engagement of the men. Every railway man now out in disregard of his contract in himself personally liable to be sued in the County Court for damages. Every trade union leader who has advised and promoted that course of action is liable in damages to the uttermost farthing of his personal possessions."

Referring to clauses in the ordinary rules of the Trade Unions that workmen would forfeit their benefits if they repudiated the orders of the Executive, he said that no Court in this country would construe such a rule as to say that a man would forfeit his benefit if he were asked to do what was wrong and illegal.

Strikers Return to Work.

Eighty-one out of 168 men employed at a Leicestershire Railway Station returned to work yesterday.

Many Great Western Railway men have returned to duty in Cardiff and in Cornwall.

Fifty transport workers have returned to duty at Halifax, and at Pudsey 170 engineers have resumed. At Armley 700 engineers have returned to work. South Shields Corporation power station workers refused to strike. Newport (Monmouth) power men have also refused to come out.

Railway men have gone back to work at Whitstable and Sittingbourne.

Lowestoft tramway employees returned yesterday, and the services will be resumed. Portsmouth members of the Electrical Trade Union have declined to obey the call-out.

JACKDAW NO. 105 GENERAL STRIKE

TO-DAY.

PUBLICITY TRIUMPHS — A CHILDISH ARGUMENT. EVERYONE HELPING—UNION LIABILITY.

Day by day publicity is triumphing over those who sought to muzzle the press in order to hide the futility of the general strike.

The newspapers could have bought permission to resume work by surrendering their independence.

They refused. They are meeting their difficulties without any aid from the surprised unions, and with steady success.

The attitude of the Parliamentary Labour Party is inexplicable.

Mr. Macdonald, in his book, clearly distinguishes between a strike in a single trade, which is an industrial dispute, and a general strike, which is an attack on the community. He and his fellow leaders, when in office, laid town again and again the duty of the Government to fight a general strike.

It is childish to contend that a general strike which was wrong when Labour was in office is permissible when Labour is in Opposition!

Yet that is Labour's argument in a sentence.

The desire of everyone to do something helpful is a wonderful response to the needs of the country. Volunteers are surging into the enrolling stations.

Mr. Bromley, the locomotive drivers' leader, recently admitted that against the full resources of the Government the strike must fail.

The Government have not yet employed anything approaching their full resources; but the strikers are already losing heart and ground.

One certain thing is, that if the dispute continues the Trade Unions will emerge bankrupted of funds and shorn of privileges.

The position of their funds cries out for amendment. It **is the height of injustice that the savings of workers contributed for pensions should be squandered against their will in strike expenditure.**

The Union leaders are liable in damages for **their illegal action in calling out the men.**

The law ought to be enforced against them.

RUSH OF VOLUNTEERS.

The number of volunteers recruited in London on Thursday was 21,085, bringing the total for London and the Home Counties to 70,180.

66 MEN REMANDED.

Sixty-six men were remanded in Glasgow yesterday in connection with the tramway depot riot at Bridgeton on Thursday night.

SOVIET OFFER TO STRIKERS.

£250,000 or a Supply of Food.

("Daily Express" Correspondent.)

New York, Friday.

It is reported here from Moscow that the Soviet Trade Union Council has offered the British strike leaders their choice between a supply of foodstuffs or a contribution of £250,000.

They calculate that it would not take longer than five days to deliver the food at English ports.

Lossovsky, the chief of the Red Trade Union International, in disclosing this offer, said the present conflict was a dress rehearsal for the time when the workers would take control.

PUBLIC MEETINGS.

Magistrates Empowered to Prohibit Them.

The House of Commons sat until 12.20 a.m. yesterday in order to pass the Emergency Regulations.

When a Socialist amendment was moved to admit the regulation giving power to prohibit public meetings, Mr. John Bromley said that on Sunday gatherings of strikers and sympathisers would be held all over the country, and the most rigorous power would not prevent them. He asked the Government to delete the regulation.

Sir Douglas Hogg, Attorney-General, stated that power given to the Secretary of State, or any magistrate or police officer authorised by him, was an essential part of the maintenance of public order.

The amendment was rejected by 299 to 89.

The Speaker stated yesterday, in reply to Col. Gretton, that the men engaged in several of the principal services of the House had been withdrawn.

"I can assure the House," he said, "that I will not allow it to be disabled from proceeding with its work by the action of any body of persons whatsoever. If it became necessary I would conduct the business of the House without any printing or without any electric light."

This declaration was greeted with cheers.

CABINET MEETING.

The Cabinet met at the House of Commons yesterday and received a report from the Chief Civil Commissioner on the situation.

Machine Gun in Paper Parcel.

Two men were arrested by the police at Sheffield for being in possession of a Lewis Machine Gun. They were carrying it through the streets wrapped in a brown paper parcel.

No Troops in Action.

An official denial was given yesterday by the Government to the rumours of the troops in action against rioters. "Not a shot has been fired, not even a blank cartridge" declared a Cabnit Minister.

PLENTY OF POWER.

All the seventy-four power stations in London except five are working satisfactorily. Battersea, Bermondsey, Stepney, Poplar and West Ham are not working normally, but there are now more than three hundred civilian volunteers helping in running the London power stations.

The King's Plans

It is the intention of the King and Queen to remain at Buckingham Palace.

The Duchess of York and her baby are still making entirely satisfactory progress.

Omnibus Services.

Services of the London General Omnibus Company with volunteer labour proceeded smoothly throughout the day. Bonnets of omnibuses were protected by wire netting. Windows were boarded up in some omnibuses. Attempts to interfere with the petrol supply to depots at Fulham and Hackney were quickly suppressed by the police.

HOSE WEAPON.

FIRE BRIGADE CLEAR A STREET.

The fir hose was turned on a mob who set fire to a lorry laden with matt cases in Page's Walk, Old Kent Road. The Fire Brigade after quenching the flames, turned the hose on the mob, and the street was cleared in thirty seconds.

A mail van, laden with income-tax papers, was overturned in the Old Kent Road and the contents scattered.

An attempt to rush the South-Eastern District Postmen's Office in Borough High Street was prevented. A large crowd surged into the courtyard, but were driven back.

CRICKET.

Cambridge University, Yorkshire at Cambridge abandoned. Final scores : Yorkshire 176 and 185 for 9. Cambridge University 176.
Essex v. Australians at Leyton delayed by rain. Australians 538 for 9 declared.
Surrey v Glamorgan at the Oval was abandoned owing to rain. Scores : Glamorgan 264. Surrey 186 for 4.
Lancashire v. Worcestershire abandoned. Final scores, Worcestershire 194 Lancashire 282 for 7.

Printed and Published by The London Daily Express Newspaper, Ltd.

PRINTED IN GREAT BRITAIN

The Observer.

(ESTABLISHED 1791)

No. 7041.　　　SUNDAY, May 9th. 1926.　　　Price 2d

LOOKING AHEAD.

Five days of the General Strike show that the Community's moral and material power of resistance has not been over-valued. The Government rightly refuses to enter into conference while the strike continues. Its determination is approved and upheld by all the leaders of the older parties in both Houses. There is quiet and unflinching support for it in every part of the land.

The General Strike has forced the constitutional issue. Obscured in its deep shadow stands the unsettled problem of the coal-fields. The strike must end before there can be any return to the problem it cannot solve. In what way will it end? It can and, if necessary, will be physically, broken by the resistance of a community determined to maintain for itself its elementary rights. If it is to be a blind struggle, enduing to that point of collapse, the economic cost will hardly be recoverable. It will also leave the marks of a permanent corrosion upon the character and temper of all political and industrial relationships. We need not pursue these clear contingencies to a further point.

The community will certainly hold out. But the struggle need not be blind. Light is still needed upon the days ahead of us. Not upon the immediate duty of the Government. That is as clear as day to the mass of the nation and cannot be less clear to the union leaders. But there are duties beyond it. It will be pertinent to know how the Government intends to use the opportunity it will have, sooner or later, when the General Strike ends. There is everything to be gained by some clear statement of the Government's intentions. The Coal Report stands. It is an economic document shaped by the facts of the coal problem. Submerged for the moment, it will reappear in due time as the only possible basis of a coal settlement. Negotiations ended without bringing the union leaders to the point of accepting or rejecting the Report. There is a strike against the Government. Is it also a strike against the report, however fairly and impartially applied? The Government would strengthen, not weaken, its hand by making such a statement as would compel the answer.

NOTICE.

Competitions, awards of prizes, and other regular features are held over.

LONDON AND THE PROVINCES

News from the country on the fifth day of the strike shows that on the whole an orderly and good-tempered spirit prevails, and local emergencies are being well met.

The most turbulent area seems to be Glasgow, where in some of the principal thoroughfares the mobs were charged by police on Friday, and the disturbances were continual during the night. Several arrests were made.

In other parts - things are generally quiet. On Thursday 4 arrests were made in Canterbury, 5 in Bath, 23 in Hammersmith and 4 in Camberwell. In connection with the latter sentences of from fourteen to four months hard labour were passed at Greenwich Police Court.

The train services everywhere are being well maintained, and the gas supply is normal.

An attack on a Berwick to Newcastle train was made at a level crossing on Friday night, stones being thrown at the engine by a crowd on either side of the train.

Regent's Park was closed yesterday morning, every entrance being guarded by Police and special constables.

The official Report of the London Fire Brigade dealing with the period from six a.m. on Thursday to six a.m. on Friday records five cases of incendiarism affecting one motor omnibus, three motor lorries and motor car.

Victoria Park has been taken over by the Military Authorities, and is now being utilised as a military encampment.

At Hull the Corporation omnibuses were brought out for the first time since Monday with young professional and business men as drivers and conductors and with a policeman on each bus. All is quiet.

Gravesend reports all quiet. The working men at Power Stations have come out, but engineers are carrying on.

Portsmouth Chamber of Commerce has passed a resolution urging the Government to take steps to prevent traders charging increased price above those prevailing on April 30th, except where the cost to them is additional.

The situation in the Black Country is quiet except for occasional Mass meetings by strikers and attempts to hold up transport with which the police are dealing effectively. The majority of works are carrying on in a manner approaching normal but coal supplies are limited in some parts.

It is stated that arrangements have been made by the trade unions with a number of electricity undertakings and that negotiations are proceeding with others. If there is a withdrawal of labour it is likely to be sectional.

THE
BRITISH WORKER

OFFICIAL STRIKE NEWS BULLETIN

Published by The General Council of the Trades Union Congress

No. 1.   WEDNESDAY EVENING, MAY 5, 1926.   PRICE ONE PENNY

IN LONDON AND THE SOUTH

Splendid Loyalty of Transport Workers

EVERY DOCKER OUT

" London dock workers are absolutely splendid," said an official of the Transport and General Workers' Union.

" So far as they are concerned, it is a 100 per cent. strike. There is no trouble and everything is going smoothly."

POLICE HELP REFUSED

At Swindon the railwaymen are obeying Mr. Cramp's injunction to remain steady and to preserve order. The Great Western works are, of course, closed, and no trains are running.

It was stated at a mass meeting of the N.U.R. that Mr. Collett (the

The General Council suggests that in all districts where large numbers of workers are idle sports should be organised and entertainments arranged.

This will both keep a number of people busy and provide amusement for many more.

chief mechanical engineer) had declined the oer of the police and the military to guard the railway works, saying he could rely on the strikers to preserve law and order. Railway workshops at Wolverton, Crewe, and elsewhere are closed.

CHANNEL SERVICES

At Dover the whole of the tramways staff are out. The cross-Channel boat service is greatly curtailed, and a large number of passengers are awaiting the opportunity to cross.

NOT ENOUGH!

From 2½ to 3 million workers have ceased work.

The Government announced by yesterday's wireless that 30,000 volunteers had registered, expressing willingness to take the strikers' places.

It doesn't seem enough!

Published for the General Council of the Trades Union Congress by Victoria House Printing Company, 2, Carmelite-street, London, E.C.4. Telephone ;8 lines): 8300 City.

WONDERFUL RESPONSE TO THE CALL

General Council's Message : Stand Firm and Keep Order

The workers' response has exceeded all expectations. The first day of the great General Strike is over. They have manifested their determination and unity to the whole world. They have resolved that the attempt of the mineowners to starve three million men, women and children into submission shall not succeed.

All the essential industries and all the transport services have been brought to a standstill. The only exception is that the distribution of milk and food has been permitted to continue. The Trades Union General Council is not making war on the people. It is anxious that the ordinary members of the public shall not be penalised for the unpatriotic conduct of the mineowners and the Government.

Never have the workers responded with greater enthusiasm to the call of their leaders. The only difficulty that the General Council is experiencing, in fact, is in persuading those workers in the second line of defence to continue at work until the withdrawal of their labour may be needed.

WORKERS' QUIET DIGNITY

The conduct of the trade unionists, too, constitutes a credit to the whole movement. Despite the presence of armed police and the military, the workers have preserved a quiet orderliness and dignity, which the General Council urges them to maintain, even in the face of the temptation and provocation which the Government is placing in their path.

To the unemployed, also, the General Council would address an earnest appeal. In the present fight there are two sides only—the workers on the one hand and those who are against them on the other.

Every unemployed man or woman who " blacklegs " on any job offered by employers or the authorities is merely helping to bring down the standard of living for the workers as a whole, and to create a resultant situation in which the number of unemployed must be greater than ever.

The General Council is confident that the unemployed will realise how closely their interests are involved in a successful issue to the greatest battle ever fought by the workers of the country in the defence of the right to live by work.

MESSAGE TO ALL WORKERS.

The General Council of the Trades Union Congress wishes to emphasise the fact that this is an industrial dispute. It expects every member taking part to be exemplary in his conduct and not to give any opportunity for police interference. The outbreak of any disturbances would be very damaging to the prospects of a successful termination to the dispute.

The Council asks pickets especially to avoid obstruction and to confine themselves strictly to their legitimate duties.

SOUTH WALES IS SOLID !

Not a Wheel Turning in Allied Industries

' MEN ARE SPLENDID !'

Throughout South Wales the stoppage is complete, and everywhere the men are loyally observing the orders of the T.U.C. to refrain from any conduct likely to lead to disturbance.

So unanimous has been the response to the call of the leaders, that not a wheel is turning in the industries affiliated to the T.U.C.

MONMOUTHSHIRE

Complete standstill of industries in the eastern valleys. Absolute unanimity prevails among the rank and file of the affiliated unions, and not a single wheel is turning in the allied industries.

Monmouth Education Authority—which has a majority of Labour representatives—has arranged to feed the school-children where required.

ABERDARE VALLEY

All railway and bus services are at a standstill. The miners' attitude indicates that they are absolutely loyal to the advice of their leaders to refrain from anything in the nature of riotous behaviour.

NEATH

The workers have unanimously responded to the call in support of the miners, and the stoppage is complete.

With one exception, safety men are remaining at their posts. The behaviour of the men is splendid.

AMMAN VALLEY

Every industry and almost the entire transport services are at a standstill at Ammanford and throughout the populous Amman Valley.

GLAMORGANSHIRE

The men are obeying implicitly the instructions of their leaders not to create any disturbance. Crowded meetings of miners have registered their unanimous intention to stand by the T.U.C.

ABERTRIDWR

At the Windsor Colliery, Abertridwr, a deputation of the men and the management met and agreed to safety men being allowed to work.

A Trades Council, composed solely of branches affiliated to the T.U.C., has been formed to act as a Lock-out Committee for Abertridwr and Senghenydd.

PORT TALBOT

Perfect order is being maintained at Port Talbot, where all the industries are shut down.

46

The British Gazette

Published by His Majesty's Stationery Office.

No. 8 — LONDON, THURSDAY, MAY 13, 1926. — ONE PENNY.

GENERAL STRIKE OFF

UNCONDITIONAL WITHDRAWAL OF NOTICES BY T.U.C.

Men To Return Forthwith.

SURRENDER RECEIVED BY PREMIER IN DOWNING STREET.

Negotiations To Be Resumed In The Coal Dispute.

WHITEHALL, May 12

The General Strike, which began at midnight on Monday, May 3, ended yesterday in an unconditional withdrawal of the strike notices by the General Council of the Trades Union Congress. The news of the settlement was conveyed to the public in the following official communiqué:—

It was intimated to the Prime Minister that the Trades Union Council desired to come and see him at Downing-street, and they arrived soon after 12 noon. Mr. Pugh made a statement, in which he stated that the Trades Union Council had decided to call off the strike forthwith.

The Prime Minister then spoke briefly. He stated that he was very glad to see that Mr. Pugh had said, and he would repeat it to his colleagues in the Cabinet.

An intimation was reached Saturday, the Prime Minister said that negotiations should be resumed, and the Government consider as to what should be done.

THE DECISION OF THE T.U.C.

NO RESUMPTION BY MINERS.

Mr. Cook And End Of The General Strike.

"Nothing To Do With Us."

Following upon a meeting of the Miners' Delegate Conference yesterday morning the following telegram was sent to all the coal-fields:—

"Miners must not resume work during the decision of Friday last at the Kingsway Hall, London, is in effect. Pumps and delegates.—Cook, Secretary."

THE KING TO THE NATION.

Appeal For Lasting Peace.

DIFFICULTIES STILL AHEAD.

"Let Us Forget Elements of Bitterness."

The King last night issued the following message from Buckingham Palace:—

TO MY PEOPLE

The Nation has just passed through a period of extreme anxiety. It was to-day announced that the General Strike had been brought to an end.

At such a moment it is supremely important to bring together all my people. Even with it such help it will be difficult, but it will not be impossible.

Let us not forget whatever elements of bitterness the events of the past few days may have created, only remembering how steady and how orderly the country has remained, though severely tried, and forthwith address ourselves to the task of bringing into being a peace which will be lasting.—GEORGE R.I.

MR. BALDWIN ON THE FINISH

Victory Of Common Sense.

STATEMENT IN PARLIAMENT.

Westminster, Wednesday.

NATURE OF THE PEACE.

Mr. Baldwin spoke so quietly that at the beginning of his statement he could hardly be heard.

THE BIRTH AND LIFE OF THE "BRITISH GAZETTE."

An Unexampled Achievement In Journalism.

HOW AN IMPROVISED NEWSPAPER REACHED A CIRCULATION OF 2,209,000.

THE GOVERNMENT ARRIVE

A FAMOUS LETTER.

Gloucester Strike Bulletin
In Conjunction with Cheltenham.

No. 7. THURSDAY, MAY 13th, 1926. PRICE ONE HALFPENNY.

This News Sheet is issued on a permit from the branch Trade Unions in the Printing Trades. It is produced entirely by voluntary labour. The "Gloucester Strike Bulletin" will be on sale each day while the dispute is in progress.

All communications and reports to be addressed to the Editors, Mr. M. P. Price and Mr. E. Bywater, at the Labour Club. A special box for the purpose and also for communications for the Council of Action has been placed in the lobby of the Club.

No. 2. May 10:26
Peaceful Picket Persuasion Points.
By CHARLES FOX.

The most significant fact that has emerged from the controversies of the past week was mentioned by Jack Hicatt from the chair at the Mass Meeting of 4,000 Gloucester Citizens on Sunday Evening. It was the disappearance of the mine owners from the stage. Condemned by commissions, by other big business interests, by the workers in the mines from chief engineer to pit boy, and by every decent thinking member of the community, these competitive, incompetent, and dog in the manger profiteers, have barred the way to progress long enough. I have been struck by the unanimity of opinion among life long Conservatives and Liberals. Labour of course has urged the solution for more than 20 years—that no public money should be spent on propping up a system based on private profit in this first essential of our national existence. Just as London found its water supply inefficiently managed by various out-of-date Company Concerns, and its myriads of citizens endangered in vitality by scanty doubtful streams of water, so London borrowed about 60 millions at 3½, bought out the shareholders, and there and then set to work to increase and purify the output. It may be noted there has been no strike, no whisper of trouble among the staff regularly employed in this same piece of Socialism. More capital is engaged than before, but the needless and inefficient mob of middlemen has been as it were superannuated, and London is not subject to threats of dear bad water when most required. Private capitalism drops out, but civic use of capital and civil servants carry on.

Well had it been for Britain if at the same date, another primary necessity of life had been dealt with nationally. Sir George Elliott, a great mining magnate, valued before the war the entire Colliery properties then at 120

millions. The British Government could have raised a loan then at 2¾, handed the owners National Certificates for the total amount, and begun just 20 years earlier to reorganise the industry. Does anyone suppose that in that period our industrial stability would have been shaken by at least 3 great lock-outs or strikes besides many local stoppages? Would the Minister of Mines in Parliament have been allowed, to whatever party he belonged, to tolerate the state of the mining villages, the yearly toll of life and limb, the imbecile waste of competitive pits, and the gap in prices between colliery and coal cellar.

This is an industrial dispute beginning with the threat to lock out the miners unless they agree to drop far below the level at which British miners can maintain their strength, and support their folks in a minimum of comfort. Once upon a time an Archbishop of Canterbury described the introduction of Chinese coolie labour to the South African mines as a "regretable necessity." There is a more Christian sense of responsibility being shewn by the leaders of the Churches to-day. Would to God these shepherds of the flock awoke earlier to the iniquities that allow such wide gulfs between the rich and poor in this wealthy land.

It began as an industrial dispute concerning colliers. It has widened out into a trial of endurance between a wonderfully solid mass of organised workers and a Government discredited even before this affair began. The trinity of industrial, political and co-operative forces is being backed also by great numbers of men and women who love justice and mercy and side for the first time in their lives with labour. These figures are interesting.

The following survive to the age of 65.

Of 1000 Clergymen 143 survive
Of 1000 Doctors 100 „
Of 1000 Building workers 43 „
Of 1000 Coal miners 18 „

Britain standing firm.

Five million Trade Unionists have answered the call and are standing firm. Millions not directly affected realise and support the great principle for which we are fighting. Authentic information is not obtained from blackleg newspapers, the British Gazette or the Broadcasting Stations. The Government with all the resources of the State at its command can publish only a two-page paper.

STOP PRESS
END OF STRIKE
Nothing Official Yet.

Wait Instructions from your Union Executives.

A message has come through by Wire 1.10 that the Strike is off. It is important, however, that all Strikers should stand firm till they receive definite instructions from their Union Executives.

OUR MOTTO MUST BE
All out together
All IN together

LATEST 3.30 p.m.
WORKERS' UNION HAVE RECEIVED OFFICIAL NOTICE THAT STRIKE ENDED.
Nevertheless strikers should wait till other Unions are officially instructed.
SLOGAN now is NO VICTIMISATION.

Cheltenham News
A REVIEW.
(From a Cheltenham Correspondent).

The great strike has now been in operation a week, and the unity among the working classes is beyond the expectations of the greatest optimist. The reports from the surrounding districts shows the position to be well maintained and even strengthened. All the efforts of the capitalist press have failed to shake the morale of the workers, and has only made the rank and file more determined than ever to prevent the gross injustice of the demands for the reduction in the miners' wages. All the preaching of the churches has failed to create the spirit of brotherhood which is being shown by all classes of the workers, and the bond of fellowship now being cemented is one which will stand the test for all time. How can these people know the feeling existing between the workers when they live their lives in the shelter of wealth and luxury and all that wealth can buy. They only know the meaning of comradeship who also know the meaning of want, and when profoundly expressed, the result leaves one gasping. The famous words of Abraham Lincoln are adaptable to the present industrial situation :—"This country cannot continue to live and to prosper half slave, half free." The crown of thorns weighing down on the brow of labour, and the crucifying of humanity on a cross of gold.

* * *

We have received a denial from the manager of the UCAL at Cheltenham that his men are out on strike. He admits, however, that a large part of his men are not working, because of transport difficulties, which only proves the effectiveness of the strike in Cheltenham.

Printed and published by James Webb Caxte Works, Hopewell Street, Glou ter.

48

In the Forest the three weekly newspapers, Cinderford's *Dean Forest Mercury*, the *Lydney Observer* and Coleford's *Dean Forest Guardian* managed to come out in abbreviated form. The newspaper operatives had no quarrel with their employers but, at the bidding of their union in London, left their jobs at the end of the working day on Monday. The Editor was able to produce his newspapers in reduced form but, having given much generous and sympathetic space to the miners and their problems in the past, he felt aggrieved that he was now so restricted. However, he continued to report trade union matters to the best of his power.

– 2 –

In most parts of the country the first day of the strike was quiet, but in the Forest they came out with enthusiasm. The effects of the rail strike were soon noticeable. At Awre station milk churns were left uncollected and at Symonds Yat, Upper Lydbrook, Coleford, Parkend, Whitecroft, Bullo Pill and Blakeney the stations were closed with the staff out in support of the miners. In Lydney six hundred tinplate workers ceased work. They were perhaps a bit too enthusiastic, however. They could not draw unemployment benefit because work was available to them but, if they had continued at their jobs until the end of the week, they could have

Whitecroft station just prior to the First World War. It closed along with other stations in and around the Forest, when station staff struck in support of the miners.

drawn it because by then the works had closed through lack of coal. Many Forest concerns were well stocked to resist shortages of fuel for some time. West Gloucestershire Power Co. had enough coal in their yard to last them for three months; Cinderford Gas Works had a three week supply.

On the second day engineers in the Gloucester area were reported to be 97 per cent out and the printing workers were solid. The same day Forest strikers were invited to the Lydney Picture House by the proprietor to see some films, but before the sweet came the serious business – John Williams

The West Gloucestershire Power Company's station at Norchard, near Lydney, had been operating for less than three years when the General Strike started and the miners' cause was not helped by the fact that there was three months supply of coal already on site. This view was taken shortly after the station opened in June 1923.

gave an up-to-date report of both local and national strike news.

On the third day the Government promised blacklegs it would prevent victimisation and ensure they lost none of their trade union benefits. Sir John Simon, a well-known politician, said the strike was illegal, and Stanley Baldwin, the Prime Minister, broadcast that *'the General Strike was a challenge to Parliament'*. Amid all the charges and counter-charges, truths, half-truths and lies that were circulating at this time, it is refreshing to read a private letter from Henry Thomas of Hampstead in London to his friend Mr Sewell in Gloucestershire, written on the third day of the strike:

'London has been too wonderful these last two days. The roads are a sight for the Gods, nothing but private cars, myriads of them . . . The trains carrying thousands of folk are handled by young fellows, smiling all the time, and without any tremor over their responsibilities. Still, what stands out in my mind are

the roads with countless cars on them and thousands of people walking in one direction in the mornings . . . and from four in the afternoon the same ceaseless ebb tide going out of London.'

On the fourth day the Government made clear it was fighting the war on the basis of what it called protecting the people from anarchy. *The British Gazette* had on its front page the following message from the Prime Minister:

Constitutional Government is being attacked, but all good citizens whose livelihood and labour have thus been put in peril bear with fortitude and patience the hardship with which they have been so thoroughly confronted. Stand behind the Government, who are doing their part, confident that you will co-operate in the measures they have undertaken to preserve the liberties and privileges of the people of these islands. The laws of England are the people's birthright. The laws are in your keeping. You have made Parliament their guardian. The General Strike is a challenge to Parliament and is the road to anarchy and ruin. **Stanley Baldwin**

But trade unionists were not impressed, and more joined the strike. Blast furnaces in the Midlands were closed down and all the workers at the electricity stations in London were now out, though some were being run by strike breakers. However, electricity to the House of Commons was cut off. The Government issued an indemnity for troops for any actions they took which they considered necessary to maintain order, an action that had ugly connotations.

In Gloucestershire more railway clerks came out. An agreement was reached between the Gloucester transport workers' union and the Gloucester Electricity Committee under which electricity from the generating station would be reduced by 50%. This meant that private houses and hospitals would have

REPERCUSSIONS OF THE STRIKE.

Maid. "What will Madam wear?"
Mistress. "Well, I really don't know. What does one wear for a strike?"

A Punch cartoon of May 1926. There was more than a hint of truth behind the joke; many in higher society looked down on the struggle and the miners.

UNDER WHICH FLAG?

Joan Bull. "ONE OF THESE TWO FLAGS HAS GOT TO COME DOWN—AND IT WON'T BE MINE."

In answer to the "British Gazette"
UNDER WHICH FLAG?

Cartoons presenting opposing points of view; on the left, John Bull, puts the establishment side, whilst the one above appeared in the pro-Union British Worker.

sufficient for their needs but factories would go short.

On the fourth day also the Archbishop of Canterbury issued proposals for a settlement. The news was printed right away by the TUC's *British Worker* but not by the Government's *British Gazette* nor broadcast by the BBC for some days. The strikers argued that the views of the Archbishop had been suppressed because he preached peace and the Government wanted war to the finish. The Archbishop's proposals were that the TUC should call off the strike, the Government should renew its offer of financial assistance to the coal industry for a short, definite, period and the owners should withdraw their new wage plan. The TUC was ready to resume negotiations at any time, though the unions were unwilling to stop the strike, but the Government said it must stop before they would negotiate. So the Archbishop's attempt at peace came to nothing.

On the fifth day armoured cars and guards in steel helmets defended a convoy two miles long carrying food from the London docks to a depot at Hyde Park. A new body of auxilliary police, called the Civil Constabulary Reserve and composed of ex-soldiers, was formed and equipped with steel helmets and truncheons. The Amsterdam Trade Union International sent a first contribution of £1,000 for strikers, which was gratefully accepted by the TUC, but later, unwilling to be accused of accepting 'Moscow gold' they returned a cheque from the Russian trade unions.

On the sixth day, a Sunday, the General Council said again they were ready to resume negotiations where they had been broken off; at High

Mass Cardinal Bourne declared that the strike was a sin against God. Meanwhile the Prime Minister showed his coolness by visiting the zoo.

On the seventh day it was clear that in the Forest, or elsewhere, very few people were abandoning the strike and returning to work, and the number of unemployed was increasing because the lack of coal and electricity meant their factories and plants could not operate. Lydney Tinplate Works was just one which was forced to close down. *The British Worker* said that in the last few days there had been 374 arrests of people causing disturbances,

Lydney Tinplate works, circa 1925. Workers here struck in support of the local miners.

over 200 in Glasgow; the BBC amplified this by announcing details of arrests and imprisonments of from three to six months for public disorder. The General Council asked for a five per cent levy from all trade unionists still in work to help those out on strike. Donations for the strikers were received from India.

On the seventh day also, Sir Herbert Samuel, Chairman of the Coal Commission, produced a memorandum he had written about the dispute. In it he suggested that the strike should be called off; the Government should subsidise the industry for a reasonable period; a national wages board should be established composed of representatives of mine workers and coal owners with a neutral member and an independent chairman; there should be no revision of the previous wage rates until the industry had been reorganised; a wage agreement should be prepared which would determine the principles on which wage rates should be fixed; and the

TO ALL WORKERS IN ALL TRADES

ADDITIONAL GUARANTEES

Official

Every man who does his duty by the Country and remains at work or returns to work during the present crisis will be protected by the State from loss of Trade Union benefits, superannuation allowances or pensions. His Majesty's Government will take whatever steps are necessary in Parliament or otherwise for this purpose.

STANLEY BALDWIN.

H.M. STATIONERY OFFICE.

JACKDAW NO. 105 GENERAL STRIKE

PRINTED IN GREAT BRITAIN

Wages Board should be empowered to adjust the rates from time to time.

Sir Herbert handed his memorandum to the Government and to the General Council on the following day and offered to mediate. His proposals were more favourable to the miners than his Commission's Report had been. The Government did not accept them but the General Council, seeking a way out of the trouble they were in, unanimously invited the miners to agree to them.

The miners flatly refused to do so. They pointed out that the Samuel Memorandum did not propose that the new national wages board should fix wage rates nationally but only that it should determine principles on which rates should be fixed in each district. Further they were not well disposed towards independent chairmen: the Samuel Report was an example of the use of an independent chairman and independent members.

The General Council, ruffled by the Federation's response, told it that they had called on all the other unions to help the miners and the miners must subject themselves to the same discipline as the rest. The Council felt that the miners should make some concession; they must not ask their fellow workers to remain on strike indefinitely on their behalf until every detail was settled to their satisfaction. The miners recognised that they could not answer such an argument, and evaded it by pointing to an equally undeniable truth that Sir Herbert Samuel had said his memorandum was no more than a statement of opinion and that '*from the outset I have been acting entirely on my own initiative, have received no authority from the Government, and can give no assurances on their behalf.*'

In the meantime, while these views were being exchanged, the strike continued. Stanley Baldwin said it was an attempt to paralyse the life of the country and had failed. The *British Gazette* tried to scare people with the headlines '*ORGANISED ATTEMPT TO STARVE NATION*', and '*THE ALTERNATIVE TO PARLIAMENTARY GOVERNMENT – FASCISM OR COMMUNISM*', and added: '*The issue now is not what the wages of miners should be, but whether democratic Parliamentary Government is to be overthrown.*'

On the eighth day the *Daily Mail* called for the arrest of members of the General Council. In Leeds and Nottingham half the textile works had closed. In Glasgow courts 100 strikers were given sentences of three months in jail and in Hull 25 received three to nine months for causing disturbances. The circulation of the *British Gazette*, according to its editor, increased as the week went on from 235,000 on the second day of the strike to 1,800,000 on the eighth.

Also on the eighth day the General Council brought out the engineers and shipbuilding workers to strengthen the strike. When the shipyard workers responded only to a limited extent, the *Gloucester Journal* said it was apparent the back of the strike had been broken and that the country as a whole was rallying splendidly to the side of law and order. But in fact the workers remained firm. Even the BBC announced that there was as yet little sign of a general collapse of the strike.

Though it was solid, it seems the TUC leaders, fearful of the Government's charge that they were were acting illegally and causing a threat to the constitution, had lost their nerve and wanted to call it off whatever the cost to the cause they had espoused. They informed the Federation that in spite of their views they intended to accept the Samuel memorandum. In reply the Federation accused them of abandoning the struggle without any guarantees from the Government. There was no certainty, they said, that if they accepted the memorandum the coal owners' lockout notices and proposed wage scales would be withdrawn and that the miners would be able to start negotiations with a clean slate at the point where they were broken off at the end of April.

The General Council ignored the protestations of the Federation and sent a delegation to Downing Street to sue for peace. J.H. Thomas told the Prime Minister the strike would be called off immediately. He made no reference to the withdrawal of the coal owners' lockout notices, or the need for the Government's public acceptance of the Samuel memorandum or the need for an undertaking which guaranteed no victimisation. He said he and his colleagues had done 'a big thing' in abandoning the strike. Ernest Bevin, one of the delegation, said they had taken a great risk in calling it off and the General Council's action must not be regarded as an act of weakness but rather one of strength. He pressed Baldwin to agree that all those who had come out on strike should be reinstated in their jobs, but received an evasive reply. The Prime Minister then said that no doubt both he and they had work to get on with. And so it was over.

In a statement to trade unions the same evening the General Council justified calling off the strike on the grounds that Sir Herbert Samuel had told them that assurances had been given that if the strike ceased a settlement could be secured. Afterwards the Council declared that the memorandum was an authorized document and constituted the terms of peace. But the falsehood would not stand: Samuel himself had said his memorandum had been written entirely on his own initiative and without any authority from the Government.

Trade unionists, local strike committees and their helpers were angry and disappointed when they heard the strike had been called off. It was as

GREAT WESTERN RAILWAY.

VICTIMISATION.

The word Victimisation has often been used in connection with Strikes. In the experience of the Great Western Railway, it has usually been imported at the end of a Strike, the Trade Unions invariably asking that there should be no victimisation. The present strike not only differs from previous strikes in that it is not associated with any dispute or Labour question affecting the Company, but because of the fact that victimisation started with the strike, the victim in this case being the Great Western Railway Company. It is indeed true to say that the Country as a whole is being victimised by a strike which is the blackest spot in the history of Labour in this country. That thousands of men with no grievance against their employers should have been "instructed" to leave work, and that so many of them should have done so passes all comprehension. It can only be explained on the ground that there was a deep conspiracy against the State. Thank God such a conspiracy cannot succeed and can only result in the discrediting of its promoters and the disillusionment of those who have been used as pawns in the game.

F. A. Cole,

General Manager.

PADDINGTON STATION,
May, 1926.

if an army had been told to retreat when it knew victory was in sight. The Catholic Church, however, was pleased at the outcome; the Cardinal Archbishop of Westminster announced that a *Te Deum* would be sung after High Mass the following day. Stanley Baldwin went on the radio and exulted about '*unconditional surrender*'; his Government extracted what revenge they could from their victory. In the following year they passed the Trades Disputes and Trade Union Act which made general strikes illegal and otherwise restricted the activities of trade unionists.

As soon as the end of the strike was announced, the employers in road and rail transport and printing disclosed plans they had prepared for wage reductions, increases in hours and open shops in their industries. Their very haste undid them. Their employees remained out on strike. Newspapers did not appear and trams, trains and buses did not run until the proposals were withdrawn.

Not all strikers went back to their old jobs at their old rate of pay. Though the Government had said they would ensure that blacklegs were not victimised, they were not prepared to do anything to prevent strikers from being victimised, given poorer jobs or lower wages, have their working conditions worsened or have their pensions reduced. They refused to compel employers to take back men and women who had been on strike, pointing out that in some cases dismissal of workers would be inevitable because of a decrease in production caused by the strike and of obligations employers had undertaken to voluntary labour. In the Forest, however, there were few cases, apart from the railways, where the employers tried to reduce wages or increase hours.

On 12 May the miners realised that the biggest display of solidarity and the greatest effort British workers had ever made had secured nothing for them. But they were determined to fight on.

The Deep Mines of Dean . . .

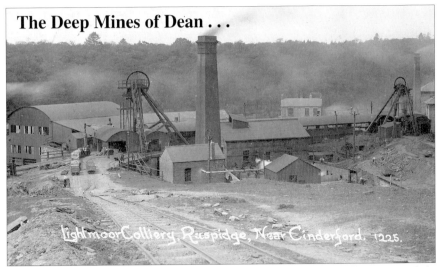

Lightmoor Colliery. Ruspidge, Near Cinderford. 1225.

Lightmoor Colliery lay in the heart of the Forest, close to the Speech House and the Dilke hospital, alongside the mineral loop line of the Severn & Wye Railway. The colliery also had its own private branch railway and locomotives, linking it with Bilson Yard, near Cinderford. It closed in 1940 after a hundred year life and is today the most intact Dean colliery site remaining, including one of the engine houses.

Eastern United Colliery, Ruspidge, Nr. Cinderford. 1190.

Eastern United was also owned by Henry Crawshay & Co. Sinking began in 1909. It was one of the easier pits to work, being a drift mine with wide, well-lit roadways, and it returned handsome profits for the company. Following nationalisation, the mine closed suddenly in 1959, much to the shock of the workforce, at a time when it was thought the location of a new seam promised it a bright future.

Yet another Crawshay pit, Foxes Bridge sat atop the escarpment looking over Bilson and Cinderford, and began producing coal in the early 1870s. In the 19th century, Foxes Bridge, Trafalgar, Lightmoor and Crump Meadow collieries, which lay within a couple of miles of one another, produced two thirds of the coal raised in Dean. Foxes Bridge closed in August 1930.

Sunk in 1824, Crump Meadow was another old colliery which did not long survive the General Strike; it closed in 1929. As with Foxes Bridge, workable reserves of coal were becoming exhausted and Crawshays were concentrating their energies on their new pit, Northern United, which opened in 1933; this pit provided employment for many who were out of work after the closure of Crump Meadow and Foxes Bridge.

Arthur & Edward Colliery or Waterloo as the men preferred to call it, lay at the head of the Lydbrook Valley. It was connected to the railway loading screens by a system of tram tubs on a half mile-long incline, operated by an endless rope and known colloquially as 'The Creeper'. The pit closed at Christmas, 1959.

New Fancy Colliery, on the hill above Parkend, employed many miners from that village following the closure of Parkend Royal Colliery. The pumps at the latter remained in operation for ventilating 'the Fancy', as it was referred to by the men. The colliery closed in 1944, despite the presence of large reserves, as it became uneconomic to work. Today, the waste heap is a noted viewpoint and the imposing stone wall of the loading bank can still be found in the woods.

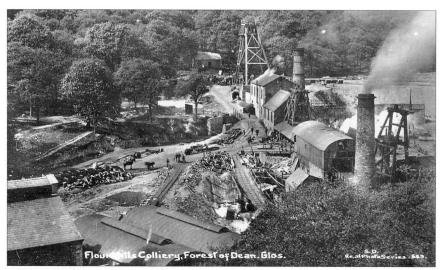

Flour Mills Colliery, Forest of Dean. Glos.

S.D.
RealPhotoSeries. 559.

Started in the 1840s, it was not until the 1860s that large-scale development began at Flour Mill Colliery, Bream. Coal was sent down a rope-worked tramway to the screens at Park Gutter (Princess Royal) for loading. The two pits were connected underground in 1916 to improve working and ventilation. Flour Mill closed in 1928 and Princess Royal in 1962. Some buildings survive, one in use by a firm repairing steam locomotives. The route of the rope-worked tramway can also be traced.

Norchard Colliery, Lydney.

Norchard Colliery was owned by Richard Thomas, owner of Lydney Tinplate works. This circa 1910 view shows the screens alongside the S&W main line into the Forest. From 1923, coal was supplied directly by conveyor to the newly opened power station nearby. By this time the pit was in the ownership of Lord Bledisloe – hence his interest in keeping the boilers stoked (see page 17). The mine closed in 1957.

THE LOCKOUT

- 1 -

The miners of the Forest of Dean suffered a blow when the end of the strike was announced. Like those in the rest of Britain they had no more security from a reduction in wages and increase in hours than they had had before 1 May. But they had endured set-backs and hardships for centuries, and the grit that had sustained them then came to the fore now. They determined to continue their struggle for higher wages and better conditions.

They met at the Speech House to lick their wounds. Bitterness ran deep. The General Council of the TUC came under attack. David Organ, the President of the Forest of Dean Miners' Association said the Council had had the full support of the whole of the trade union movement of the country behind them but they had got the wind up and had perpetrated this colossal and disastrous betrayal. John Williams, the miners' agent, accused the Council of even greater treachery. Before Sir Herbert Samuel had issued his memorandum there had, he understood, been private discussions behind the scenes between the TUC's negotiating team and Samuel, without the presence or knowledge of the Miners' Federation. And the General Council had represented these purely private conversations as a basis of settlement! It was all an excuse for a cowardly surrender. But, Williams went on, it was not only the miners who had been betrayed; the transport workers and the dockers had been let down, too. They had fought valiantly for the miners and now they were humiliated. But the miners would not give in, said Williams: '*They can bring troops and police here, with their batons and their guns, but they cannot* make *us go down Lightmoor or Foxes Bridge or the Princess Royal.*'

Almost immediately after the end of the strike Stanley Baldwin made proposals to both the coal owners and the miners to end the lockout, but neither side found them acceptable. The miners realised they now faced a long and lonely struggle. No-one knew when or how it would end. During the first few weeks the lack of earnings did not show itself, since they drew their wages up to the end of April. But after that they had to use their

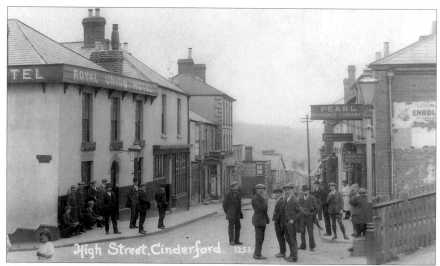

High Street, Cinderford, early 1920s, possibly during one of the strikes. The Royal Union Hotel, now demolished, was a miners' pub, where the men would meet up outside work to drink and socialise; this photograph shows quite a number of miners in their 'off duty' wear, gathered in and around the pub for a chat.

savings and then seek credit from the shops.

The funds of the Forest of Dean Miners' Association were so reduced that it could not give any lockout pay. However, the Federation distributed some benefit: 5s for each man, 1s for his wife and each child and 2s 6d for a youth. More was promised later but the Federation said it would be less than on this occasion and those who received poor law relief would not get anything. Later a miners' distress fund was set up to which other trade unions and private individuals contributed. The major contributors were the Russian trade unions. There was also a local distress fund to which those in work contributed. In addition to the school dinners provided by the County Council, soup kitchens were organised in the villages. Mrs Deakin the wife of Thomas Hedges Deakin, owner of the Parkend and New Fancy collieries, helped to organise one at Parkend. It was ironical that the wife of a coal owner should give succour to people reduced to hunger by her husband.

All this assistance was no substitute for a regular wage, small and inadequate though that might be. Sooner or later many miners had to apply for poor law relief from the Boards of Guardians at Westbury, Monmouth and Ross-on-Wye, which served the Forest area. The rules for outdoor poor law relief stipulated that where an applicant was able-bodied and physically capable of work, he could not be granted relief if work was available, though his dependants could be helped if they were destitute. Even if they gave relief, the Westbury Board would not grant it for more than two weeks, at the end of which period the matter must be considered further. They also insisted that the money was a loan not a gift, and wanted it back when the lockout was over. By the middle of May the Board were granting relief of over £500 a week, and were concerned with the cost if the lockout continued much longer, because their income was declining; many ratepayers were being excused their rates and the collieries, who were assessed mainly on output, were not contributing much either.

An interesting member of the Westbury Board was a miner, C.E. Mason, known generally as Charlie Mason. He was a fervent union supporter, a left-wing member of the Labour Party and a member of the East Dean Rural District Council. He was well-known and well-loved, and was still remembered affectionately in Dean fifty years after his death. Charlie Mason harried the other members of the Board relentlessly on the subject of outdoor relief for the locked-out miners. He urged them to be generous where they had discretion, and not only to preach the principle of brotherhood but to practise it as well.

Initially they had decided that the weekly allowance for a wife should be 10s (about £17 in 1999), with 4s for the first child and 2s 6d for subsequent children. When, even before payments had started, they decided

The Speech House circa 1930. This is the centre of the Forest and was the focal point for generations of Dean miners, particularly at times of industrial strife. Many meetings were held under the surrounding trees, a sylvan spot yet witness to much anger.

C.E. 'Charlie' Mason, a miner, a member of the Westbury Board of Guardians and a stalwart champion of the locked-out miners. He was the father of celebrated Forest author Winifred Foley.

to reduce the allowance for the first child to 2s 6d, Mason told them they appeared to be taking sides against the miners, whereas they were expected to be impartial. He said that the low levels of relief they were granting did not even achieve the theoretical aims for relief set out by the Government, which was the relief of destitution. He queried their motive in making the relief a loan and not a gift. He pointed out the foolishness of issuing all the relief in the form of food vouchers, and moved, without success, that 25 per cent should be given in cash. He attempted to shame them for taking into account the odd pound in the Co-op bank, withdrawn to keep body and soul together. He argued against the deduction of the 'Russian Money' – a gift from Russia to help British miners in their struggle – from their relief.

He was equally vocal in urging the Board to exceed the limits laid down by the Government. He argued the case for an allowance for single men with such vehemence that the Chairman refused to let him continue and told him '*You are doing your case more harm than good by pursuing this matter*'. In all these confrontations Charlie was supported by a few other stalwarts but out of a Board of about thirty he and his fellows were usually in a minority of five.

The Monmouth Board of Guardians were equally tight. They decided that single men, even if they were buying their own houses and were burdened with mortgages, could not be helped. However, they were prepared to pay 10s a week for a wife and 3s for each child up to a maximum of 25s (about £43 in 1999). But the children, the Board were informed,

"Feed the Children Movement" May 17th 1926.

Donations :—

	Money & Goods	Expenditure

Donations :—

	£		
Mr E. J. Flewelling	1	0	0
Mr Gilbert Yemm	2	0	0
Mr A.T. Cooper	10	0	0
The Labour Whist Club		15	0
Cinderford Onward Band	5	2	6
Old Schools Whist Club		7	8
Mr A. Turner		2	6
Wesleyan Childrens Operata		3	3
Collection R.A.O.B. Lodge Cinderford	4	6	
A.W. Manning Esq, Cinderford	1	1	0
Mr W.A. Morris		10	0
Labour Whist Club		15	6
W. Davies Esq., Ross		1	0
Arthur & Edward Band with Phil	6	6	
Old School … Whist Club		5	6
Miss Toomb., S. Hills, S. Foxwell with Bazar at Whitehurst		9	0
Mr Llywelyn F. Baxter		2	8
Collection (Mountjombs Mitcheldean) & Phil		10	0
Mr Jas C. Martin		17	8½
Trafalgar Cheddveigh Fund part Mr E.A. Phelps		5	0
Mrs Townsend Sen.		10	0

Money & Goods

- Mr E. J. Parsons … 12 lbs Beef
- M.A. Turner … 2 galls of Milk
- Mr M. Hamblin … 1 cwt Coal
- Mr A. Turner … 1½ galls Milk
- Mr J. Wheatstone … 5 cwt Coal
- Mr Frank Toomb., Hauling 4 cwt Potatoes
- Rev C.A. Hopkins … 2 cwt Potatoes
- Mr Donald Bradley ½ galls Milk and Leonard Collins
- Biscuits …
- Arthur & Edward Colliery Co. … 1 cwt Coal
- Mr G.T. Bishop … 72 eggs
- Rev G. A. Hopkins
- Mr … lb
- Mr A.T. Cooper, Ball Hotel 2 cwt Potatoes
- Mrs O. Phelps 6 lb plts of Graden Oats, 8 small loaves
- Mr W. Davies Ros, Davis Potatoes
- Miss Burgum 6 jars of Harris Paste
- Mr Clifford Jones carried 2 cwt potatoes from Ross
- Arthur & Edward Colliery, 4 cwt Coal
- Mr W. Robinson … 2 Bristol Potatoes
- Mr N. A. Bennett … Sack of Cabbages.

Expenditure.

	£	s	d
T. Morgan Potatoes Hauling	1	14	0
H.J. Barrett … Peas Sheb		16	4
E. J. Parsons … further Beef		14	0
M. A. Burgum		7	11½
F. Gibbs. Bread 4/- 8/9 6/-		15	6
A.T. Beard. Bread 4/9 6/-		12	9
Williams + Cohen		7	7½
N.J. Meredith. Bread		9	9
O. Phelps. Bread		2	4½
O. Phelps 5/10½ 2/3 16½		9	0
M.A. Burgum 11/2½ 6/- 15/2½		14	0
F. Gibbs ½		13	2
N.J. Meredith ½		12	1
Williams + Cohen		6	6½
A.T. Beard		6	4
E.T. Parsons		6	4
J. Black Potatoes	4		
E. J. Parsons		18	9
T. Morgan Potatoes		4	4½
Leonard Collins		5	3
H. J. Barrett		4	8½
N.J. Meredith		4	4
O. Phelps		2	2½
A.T. Beard Bread 6/- 4/-		12	0
F. Gibbs 6/- 2/9		4	7
M.A. Burgum		2	8
Williams + Cohen		4	11
E. J. Parsons	1	15	4½
W. J. Meredith		11	6
M. A. Burgum		10	7
Williams + Cohen		17	5
G …		12	1

Part of an account sheet for the Forest's 'Feed the Children Movement'.

"While the miners are our enemies we should not feed them. We did not feed the Germans, and I cannot for the life of me see why we should feed the miners."—Lord Hunsdon.

As the strike progressed and the conflict became more bitter, the satirical cartoons developed even more of a harder edge and lost what little humour they had possessed. The drawing *above* appeared in The Miner *in September 1926 and showed Pontius Pilate washing his hands of a Jesus Christ representing the miners, whilst the crowd bay for blood.*

The cartoon *left*, from the Daily Worker, *was even more stark, showing a fat capitalist owner happy to starve the miners' children to death. The caption refered to one politician's view comparing the miners to the Germans during World War 1.*

received a free dinner at school every day including Sunday (worth 5d), paid for by the county education authority, and some Board members attempted, unsuccessfully, to have the 5d a day taken into consideration when granting relief for the children.

On June 11, in the sixth week of the lockout, a contingent from the Forest of about 90 men arrived at the Board's offices at Monmouth. They were nearly all single men, many of them weak from malnutrition, and had tramped the ten miles from Bream to put their case to the Board for relief. Four of the men were invited into the Board room. Their spokesman said there was more destitution in the Forest than there had been in the 1921 lockout and some men were starving. Many single men were in lodgings and needed money to pay their landladies, but even if they still lived at home they were in effect lodgers. Those who had managed to save a little when in work – and they were few – had by now spent their savings.

The Chairman of the Board said single men could not be relieved unless they were physically unfit and had a medical certificate to prove it. A Board member from the Forest said that, if they wanted to, the Board could interpret the rules so that single men not physically unfit could be given relief and there was a long wrangle on the subject. Feelings ran high; one member made a remark which was interpreted by another as saying 'Starve them into submission' but it was denied; all she had meant was 'Let them go back to work and get money'. Finally it was resolved to ask the Ministry of Health, who operated the poor law arrangements, for power to be more generous and enable them to give relief to able-bodied men.

The men outside were told of the decision and offered a meal of bread and cheese if they left the premises, but they decided to stop and press their demands. When they realized the Board would not yield, they left. As they did so their spokesman said 'These men will not go under lightly. They have had enough burying underground. They are prepared to starve on top, and they will gladly let you bury them.' One man was heard to add 'If we have to die, let us die here.'

– 2 –

In June efforts were again made nationally to bring together the two sides involved in the lockout so that the deadlock might be broken and a solution thrashed out, but nothing definitive emerged until July when, in a step that was clearly intended to force a solution on the miners, Parliament passed the Coal Mines Act under which the miners' working day could be increased from seven hours to eight. The Forest of Dean Colliery Owners' Association, along with the other colliery owners nationally, now announced that their pits would be open from 12 July on new terms and conditions. The hours would be eight per shift, with seven on Saturdays. The rates of pay per shift would be broadly the ones obtaining before

the lockout, but would be reviewed after $11^1/_2$ weeks.

John Williams was concerned that some of his men might return to work on the new terms. He held a meeting at the Speech House and launched an attack on any men thinking of returning, urging members to stay loyal to the Federation. He pointed out that before the lockout wages for a face worker were 8s 3d (about £14 in 1999) for a seven hour working day and under the employers' new proposals they would be the same for an eight hour day. This was the equivalent of a reduction of 12 per cent in pay. All contractors and piece rate workers would similarly be reduced by 12 per cent and surface men would also get a reduction.

He urged them not to go back on these terms and the men had little inclination to do so. It seems that, if forced to choose, they would have accepted a drop in wages rather than an increase in hours, if only because an increase in hours would mean more unemployment.

Pressure to accept the new terms was exerted on the miners by Ramsay MacDonald and some other members of the Labour party leadership. They held the view that the miners should have accepted the Coal Commission's proposals, ignoring the fact that the owners had shown a disposition to accept only part of them. Some of the leadership also made attacks on the Federation, claiming that something other than a long strike was needed to solve the colliers' problems with all its attendant hardships for them and their families. A.A. Purcell, the Forest MP, even said the miners should accept a reduction in wages in the interests of the trade union movement as a whole.

A sign that the employers did not think the men were ready to return was the decision at Lightmoor to bring up the horses. In fact in only a few of the large collieries did many men return to work. At Eastern United 206 went back, at Norchard 47 and at New Fancy 20. None went back at Cannop, Flour Mills or Princess Royal.

While at this time there were a few demonstrations against colliers who remained at work or went back after coming out, there was no violence. One otherwise militant miner said that the number returning to work was not enough to make it worth while demonstrating and risking going to Gloucester Gaol for. It was the men in the little pits in the Forest, quite out of proportion to their numbers, who caused many of the demonstrations that arose. These pits numbered about 40 and employed between them about 1,000 men. Even though they claimed that in the main they supported the union, they weakened the solidarity of the miners by remaining in work. They argued they were justified in not coming out because if they had they would lose their jobs to outsiders and not be able to get them back when the dispute was over.

Even John Williams the miners' agent, who was always on the lookout for any degree of blacklegging, must have been amused at the happenings at the True Blue Colliery at Ruardean where two members of the same family resumed work on the old rates and hours. In protest someone broke the top off a fruit tree belonging to one of them, with the result that two more members of the family went back to work in defiance. Police hurried to the scene, but trouble was averted when the four men left work again on being promised that the damage to the tree would be paid for. The colliery was then idle once more.

View of Ruardean circa 1930. On the right can be seen the waste tip of True Blue Colliery, one of the many small mines which proliferated in Dean.

The Small Mines of Dean . . .

A view of the Coleford to Cinderford road in the 1930s. Cannop Foundry can be seen just down the road, with the Hopewell Colliery site in view beyond. Still working today, it has now also been turned into the Hopewell Colliery Mining Museum and visitors can take trips underground. In the centre distance, Speech House Hill Colliery can also be seen; by this date it was in use purely for pumping water out of Lightmoor.

An Albion bus belonging to Red & White, who operated services around the Forest from depots at Cinderford and Lydney, seen waiting at Yorkley. The local Red & White men also came out in support of the miners. Behind the bus is a glimpse of Thornton Reeks Colliery; the waste tip and some empty trams can be seen.

The New Regulator Pit at Heywood, near Cinderford, was another small mine. Many of the employees of the small mines stopped work initially but soon went back as the privations of the lockout took hold. This lack of support did much to undermine the resolve of the miners in the bigger pits and was one of the main reasons why Forest solidarity was not as strong as in the other coalfields.

Nor was Williams too worried about the situation at the small Thornton Reeks colliery at Oldcroft, where all the colliers returned to work but on a seven not an eight hour basis; or at Hopewell Drift where the fourteen men there also returned under the old arrangments of a seven hour day and the old rates of pay.

However, as time went on some ugly incidents arose when the pressures of hunger and despair grew and the animosity of the men who were out against those who remained in work began to increase. At the Ruffit (between Littledean and Cinderford) the windows at the home of a man who had returned to work were smashed. There was trouble at the small Fryer's Level near Whitecroft where an angry crowd of about 200 men, women and children waited for colliers coming off shift at 2 o'clock in the afternoon and greeted them with shouts of 'blacklegs', boos and jeers, and the rattling and banging of old kettles, buckets and tins with sticks. This was known as 'tanging' and was used widely to show disapproval of blacklegging. Tanging was an old tradition in the Forest but usually reserved for showing approval at weddings.

The scene was repeated when the next shift left work at 9 pm. The crowd now numbered about 300 and had been joined by a woman with a

Two photographs showing police escorting miners to work at Cinderford. There was a certain amount of intimidation, or 'tanging' as it was referred to in the Forest, involving mainly slanging or stone throwing but, apart from the odd nasty incident, the Dean was fortunate not to suffer the worst excesses of such behaviour, as other areas did. In some coalfields, the legacy of bitterness caused by blacklegs has lasted to this day, being passed down the generations. Forest miners generally seem to have been a little more philosophical towards those who felt they could not hold out. At the end of the day, Foresters tended to stick together, come what may. The group above look quite cheerful and not at all intimidated, whilst the two policeman follow at a discreet distance.

melodeon. As they emerged from the pit the men tried to go home but two of them were surrounded by protesters who threw turf at them. The same happened when the men left home for work the next day. That evening they were given a police escort home, but the crowd, undeterred by the presence of the constabulary, followed and continued their demonstrations. It seems that only three of the ringleaders of the demonstration were arrested and taken to court. They were found guilty and bound over for twelve months in a bond of £10.

Other cases of intimidation included a group of thirty or forty men who waylaid a man cycling to work on his bike and threw stones at him. Six men were arrested for this. The magistates discharged one of them and fined the other five. Later, True Blue Colliery at Ruardean was in the news again. As three men left work late one night and were going through the village they met a large crowd of thirty or forty people who began to hoot at them and shout 'blacklegs' and throw stones. The three men were accompanied by a police escort who ordered the crowd to disperse. When they did not, they arrested five of them. In court the five denied throwing stones or shouting 'blacklegs'. One said he had been at choir practice, another that he had just been leaning against the church wall. They produced witnesses to support their innocence. One witness said the chorister had indeed been at choir practice all the evening and another that the man who claimed he had been leaning up against the church wall had been doing just that – *doing nothing and doing it well* – but the bench found them all guilty.

In the House of Commons the Home Secretary said he was aware that in the Forest of Dean there had recently been a number of cases of intimidation against miners who wished to work, and proceedings had been instituted in some sixty cases. The strength of the police had been considerably increased there, he said, but all the extra men – foot police from Gloucester and mounted police from Cheltenham – had not been needed. He was right; there was no need for police protection at five of the big collieries and the extra police detailed had been able to go to Cinderford to a football match between strikers and the police.

In August the Forest of Dean Miners' Association organised a demonstration in Cinderford against blacklegs, especially against the increasing

FOOTBALL.

Gloucester Strikers
v.
Forest of Dean
TO-DAY (MONDAY) at 3 o'clock
on
Sisson Road Grouud

Admission 2d.
Proceeds for Relief Fund.

Gloucestershire Constabulary Mounted Police, photographed in the yard at the rear of the now demolished Feathers Hotel in Lydney in July 1926. Brought in from Cheltenham to control intimidation, they were not really required as the situation in the Forest never got out of control.

For the duration of the strike in the Forest, the police were under the control of Superintendent Shelswell. He was billeted at Tutshill House (the bottom of Highfield Hill in Lydney) and was driven round the Forest in a Chevrolet tourer. Locals familiarly referred to him as 'Super' Shelswell.

number of men returning to work at Eastern United and Lightmoor. Headed by David Organ the president of the Association, John Williams its agent, A.A. Purcell the MP, and the town band, they marched round Cinderford and assembled at the Co-operative Society's field in the town centre for an open-air meeting. David Organ referred to '*those black scabs who were assisting the coal owners*' and John Williams said he thought blacklegging was '*the vilest thing he could conceive of.* Blacklegs, he said, would carry with them a stigma of the worst kind as long as they lived. He himself would feel like a criminal if he had to be helped to work by policemen. All this meant that they must intensify their picketing and cut down the blacklegging.

Three days later another meeeting was held in Cinderford. On this occasion John Williams sadly reported that in spite of all their efforts, the number of men returning to Eastern United and Lightmoor was increasing. Pickets were at the collieries every day but there were not enough of them to do the job properly. He appealed for 500 volunteers to help existing pickets at pit heads. He also thought pickets should accompany the blacklegs from home to pit and argue with them peacefully on the way so as to maximise their inconvenience – attacking their consciences twenty times a week might help. But there should be no intimidation or conflict with the police.

Another form of blacklegging was happening with ever increasing frequency in the Forest: outcropping – raising coal from outcrops and scavaging on tips and dumps. The men who did this paid, where

Womens Committee for the Relief of Miners Wives and Children.

They need your help!

In the coalfields, hundreds of children are born every week into houses where dire poverty reigns. The mothers are weakened by anxiety and under-nourishment. They are often without baby clothes, and they have no money to buy them; they lack proper clothing and bedding for themselves. We are trying with your help to send them food and clothing, soap and other necessaries.

In many a home there is not a penny to pay for light, so that the sick children cannot be properly tended at night.

The little children are running on the rough roads with broken boots or barefooted, their soft feet cut by the stones.

There is not enough money to get the young ones fresh milk, and the sudden heat wave will bring the dreaded summer sickness, the scourge of ill-fed little ones, in its train.

Will you help us to provide for these small children and their mothers?

JACKDAW NO. 105 GENERAL STRIKE

appropriate, a nominal sum to the Crown for the right to take the coal. It was often of the poorest quality and had been long ago cast aside as of no marketable value. So much was being raised in some parts of the Forest that it was difficult to find transport for it all. The reward from outcropping was substantial; it was said four men had made £60 between them in a week. The resolve of many men not to return to work was weakened by the activities (and income) of these outcroppers.

– 3 –

Meanwhile miners continued to apply for outdoor relief for their wives and families at the three Boards of Guardians that served the Forest. At Westbury, where about 750 people were receiving relief, members of the Board complained that many of the collieries were open and the men could go back to work if they wished, and that while they received relief they would not go back. There was no sign their refusal to go to work was coming to an end and the granting of so much relief was putting a strain on the Board's resources and thus placing a heavy burden on the ratepayers. This was resented, they said, especially in the agricultural areas where a labourer's weekly wage was 30s (about £51 in 1999) with six or seven to keep. By carrying on paying they were only prolonging the strike. Their big mistake had been to pay any relief in the first place. Charlie Mason, who was a member of the Board, and his small core of dissidents disagreed violently, but the Board decided to pay no more relief unless proof was supplied by a man's colliery that work was not available for him there.

That decision launched a protest that the Board had not foreseen. A crowd of 300 men and 150 women and children assembled outside the workhouse. Many had walked as far as 7 or 8 miles. Police present guarded the building and were on the lookout for riotous behaviour but they were unnecessary; the crowd was orderly, indeed good-humoured. Led by the women they sang *"Guide me, O thou Great Jehovah"*, emphasising the line '*Bread of Heaven! Feed me till I want no more.*' This was followed by *"Lead Kindly Light"*, *"Don't go down the Mine, Daddy"* and *"The Red Flag"*.

The Board, who had assembled inside the building for their weekly meeting, found the noise prevented them from discussing their business and some wanted to abandon the meeting. Charlie Mason was sitting in his place and no doubt enjoying the music from outside. He rose and insisted on making a speech. He could hardly be heard, the *Mercury* reported, but the words, '*The Board have only got what they asked for*', came over clearly.

Westbury on Severn circa 1920. The workhouse administered by the Westbury Board of Guardians lay down a lane to the right of where the photographer was standing.

The Board maintained their decision to refuse relief, so Charlie and John Williams, the miners' agent, conceived a plan. They advised the wives to seek admission to the workhouse by obtaining the necessary orders from the Relieving Officer. This the women did, and assembled early one morning at Cinderford. There were 296 women and children, some babes in arms, and they were taken by chartered motor buses to Westbury. Here they knocked politely on the door of the workhouse, handed in their orders and were admitted by the Master. After they had all been given dinner, some two dozen decided to return to Cinderford, walking all the way, but 270 remained. The next day, after spending a night in the workhouse, these women walked back with their children to Cinderford. Here Charlie took them into the Town Hall where they were greeted by miners cheering them for the heroines they were.

Accounts of what happened during the women's overnight stay differ. According to the women the food was uneatable and the accommodation they were offered unacceptable. According to the Master the women threatened the staff, trampled on mattresses, tore up pillow slips and refused to empty their slops. Further, they were rowdy, sang all night, and upset the long-term inmates.

The Master gave his version at the next Board meeting. Charlie denied its accuracy, though he accepted that to have nearly 300 would-be paupers descend on the workhouse all at once was a challenge. The cost of the invasion, he told the Board, had been more than the cost of a week's relief. Westbury, he said, was the only Board of Guardians in the United Kingdom that refused to pay relief to locked-out miners' dependants. He had sympathy for the ratepayers but pointed out that in 1914 plenty of money could be found to blow out people's brains and nobody had cried out about taxation then. Anyway, since the Board had insisted that the relief was only a loan they would get their money back in due course. But the Board were not moved by his arguments and would not change their policy.

To demonstrate against the Board's decision two processions of miners converged at the Co-operative Society's field in Cinderford and held a protest meeting. One was from Cinderford itself and was headed by the town band; the other was from Drybrook, which also had its brass band at the head. John Williams said he thought the Westbury Board of Guardians' decision to stop relief was illegal. There was in fact strong legal support for what they had done. As a result of their action, he said, a large number of families would starve. He advised men who were in distress to apply for tickets from the relieving officer to enter the workhouse. Shortly afterwards the Ross Board of Guardians stopped giving relief to miners' wives and children, and there was then no relief from any of the Boards that served the Forest. Distress in the district reached a level hitherto unknown; women and children were undoubtedly starving.

The bishops of the Church of England and leaders of the free churches now entered the arena. They declared that the fight between the two sides was a moral one as well as an economic one, and through the Industrial Christian Fellowship put to the Federation suggestions how the conflict could be ended. The two parties met and agreed there should be a return to work on the old terms with arbitration on wages after four months. These proposals were put to a special delegate conference of the Federation who recommended the branches to accept them. If accepted, the bishops and leaders of the free churches undertook to take the proposals to the Prime Minister suggesting they should form the basis of fresh negotiations.

A.J. Cook, the Federation secretary, warned miners that if the Federation rejected the Church's proposals there was likely to be a considerable increase in the number of men returning to work, since many men who were thinking of returning had delayed in case the proposals bore fruit. But the delegates to the conference, to the surprise of their leaders, turned the proposals down. The big mining areas in Lancashire, Yorkshire and South Wales overwhelmed the other, smaller, districts which were broadly in favour. The Forest of Dean district, however, was also against, being suspicious of arbitration and suspecting that it was likely to lead to a reduction in pay.

By August the hardship and suffering of the miners and their families was considerable. Colliers were often arrested and brought to court for stealing coal. One man from Mile End was charged with stealing coal valued at 3s (about £5 in 1999) from a railway wagon owned by the Lydney & Crump Meadow Coal Co. When challenged in Court his eyes filled with tears. He said he had only taken the coal to sell it to have some food. He had not had any that day. The Chairman of the magistrates said it was not the first time he had stolen coal and fined him £1 with the option of seven days in gaol.

Desperate for relief the Federation sent delegations to the USA, Europe and the Soviet Union to raise funds to relieve their members. Up to the present the Government had not interferred with the collection of relief, but now a message from Stanley Baldwin was published in the United States saying that there was no hardship or destitution among the miners. The message caused uproar in trade union circles and among many of the public. It was obviously timed to coincide with the Federation delegates' seeking funds in America.

In the 15th week of the lockout, in mid-August, it was estimated that in the Forest the number of men employed in the principal collieries who had returned to work (excluding the safety men who numbered about 550) was:

Lightmoor	272
Eastern United	260
Norchard	75
Oldcroft	43
Waterloo	28
New Fancy	15
New Regulator	14
Slope, Drybrook	13
TOTAL	720

At the Flour Mill, Princess Royal, Parkend Deep, Cannop and Crump Meadow collieries no men had returned.

A fortnight later the total of men who had returned had gone up to 850. By the 20th week, 200 or more men had returned to the Princess Royal and the total figure was 1,754. By the 21st week the number working had gone up to 2,349. Of these as many as 560 had returned at Eastern United (where the normal complement was 900) and a second shift had been introduced there. In addition to the overall number of men who had returned to work, 288 had signed on but had not started because the pits

Facts for Miners.

In the last three months of last year (excluding the subsidy) nearly three quarters of our Coal was produced at a loss.

THE DISTRICT LOSSES

SCOTLAND SOLD 7,932,000 TONS. OF THIS 6,980,160 TONS WERE SOLD AT A LOSS.

DURHAM SOLD 7,570,000 TONS. OF THIS 7,342,000 TONS WERE SOLD AT A LOSS.

YORKSHIRE, NOTTS, DERBY, CANNOCK CHASE, LEICESTERSHIRE AND WARWICKSHIRE SOLD 20,000,000 TONS. OF THIS 9,823,000 TONS WERE SOLD AT A LOSS.

NORTHUMBERLAND SOLD 3,039,000 TONS. ALL AT A LOSS.

SOUTH WALES AND MONMOUTH SOLD 9,997,000 TONS. OF THIS 8,997,300 TONS WERE SOLD AT A LOSS.

LANCASHIRE, CHESHIRE AND NORTH STAFFS SOLD 5,415,000 TONS. OF THIS 3,844,650 TONS WERE SOLD AT A LOSS.

The average loss on each Ton of this Coal was 1/5½.

THE MINERS' LEADERS HAVE TURNED DOWN EVERY SUGGESTION DESIGNED TO MAKE GOOD THE ABOVE LOSSES.

The Miners' Leaders have turned down these 7 proposals:

THE SEVEN REFUSALS

1. THE REPORT OF THE COMMISSION.
2. THE OFFER OF A FURTHER £3,000,000 TO EASE THE TRANSITION.
3. THE ORIGINAL TERMS OF THE OWNERS FOR A 7-HOUR DAY.
4. THE SAMUEL MEMORANDUM.
5. THE GOVERNMENT'S PROPOSALS.
6. THE KNOWN WISHES OF THE TRADE UNION CONGRESS GENERAL COUNCIL.
7. THE AMENDED WAGE OFFERS OF THE OWNERS FOR AN 8-HOUR DAY.

The Coal Industry cannot work at a loss.

There cannot be any further subsidy in any circumstances.

THE MIDLANDS CHOOSE

Thousands of Miners in the Midlands are daily bringing this Policy of blank refusal to an end. They have found Local Solutions, and are back at work and wages. Every Miner everywhere must sooner or later face the facts--and return to work.

For Your Family's Sake--For Your Own Sake--For Your Fellow Trade Unionists' Sake--For Your Country's Sake--

GO BACK TO WORK.
The Choice is Yours!

were not ready to absorb them after their long period of idleness.

Signs now apppeared that the employers were getting confident the men would return in greater numbers. Horse-shoeing at the colliery blacksmiths was given top priority, stores were replenished and a wagon-load of new shovels arrived at Whitecroft Station.

In the country as a whole men were also drifting back but not to the extent that they were in the Forest. Estimates varied but it was thought that nationally between 50,000 and 100,000 had returned – between 5% and 10% of the total work force.

– 4 –

At the end of September A.J. Cook, the general secretary of the Miners' Federation, came to the Forest and addressed a crowd of over 3,000 at the Speech House. Much of his speech was devoted to attacking blacklegs, men, he said, who were stabbing their mates in the back and prolonging the battle. He attacked duplicity:

'There is not a word in the English language that can fittingly describe a man who will come here and applaud and shout "Cook, don't give in", and who tomorrow will call on the manager of the colliery office for work. When I meet the Prime Minister and tell him our men will not accept longer hours, I am told that in the Forest of Dean there are men working eight hours at reduced wages. I have been made a liar by every single man who has gone back. I say to the man who will go to the pit and tell his manager one thing and tell his leader another he is not worthy to be among honourable men.'

Cook said that the Forest of Dean was the only coalfield in the South to break away. Kent, Wales, Bristol and Somerset continued to be solid to a man. In conclusion he said *'not a penny off the pay, not a minute on the day'* was their aim now as it had been in April: *'The battle will not be won in London but in the collliery villages, in the soup kitchens and in the homes of the men who have made history in 1926.'*

It was a masterly speech, but it did not stem the return to work in the Forest, and blacklegging continued to be a problem there. Although Federation headquarters considered Dean to be of little importance because of its small number of miners – the Forest had 6,500 in the bigger pits compared, for example, with South Wales's 216,000 – they designated it a 'black' area, though not as black as Leicestershire, where the local union had advised a return to work and 90% of the men had gone back. The Executive of the Federation sent emissaries to Dean who took over control from John Williams and his Executive and tried hard to bring out again the men who had already gone back to work. Their efforts were unsuccesful and the emissaries went back.

At the end of October the number signing on at the bigger collieries was 3,866. This, with the 550 safety men, meant that 4,416 miners were working, which compared with 6,520 employed on 1 May at the beginning of the lockout.

John Williams's position was a difficult one. He still had a solid core of miners who supported him in his aim of securing as good rates of wages and hours as prevailed the previous April but he also had in membership the large number, nearly two thirds of his members, who had returned to work, not because they no longer supported the Federation's demands but because they felt they couldn't hold out any longer. There was, of course, some resentment and ill-feeling between the two groups but on the whole a surprisingly tolerant spirit existed between them. The men at work attended union meetings as freely as those not at work. Indeed they voted on whether the various offers should be accepted or not. John Williams retained the confidence of both sides.

Even though the degree of blacklegging in the country was still fairly small it was growing, and the Federation realised they must moderate their demands. They now asked the Government to convene a meeting of the owners, the Government and themselves. '*We are prepared,*' they wrote, '*to enter into negotiations for a new national agreement with a view to a reduction in labour costs to meet the immediate necessities of the industry.*' On

Strikers meeting at the Speech House in 1926, being addressed by A.J. Cook.

seeing the words '*reduction in labour costs*' the Government contacted the owners, and as a result new Government proposals emerged. There should be a general resumption of work, local district discussions on hours and pay, and a National Arbitration Tribunal to review any settlements under which more than seven hours a day were to be worked.

The Federation Executive did not like the proposals. The Government, they concluded, wanted to abandon national negotiations and agreements (which the Samuel Commission had favoured) and replace them by local negotiations and agreements. But they knew they had to choose between either accepting the proposals or carrying on in the knowledge that by now over a quarter of the miners in the country had gone back, and that sooner or later the slow drift back to work might become an avalanche. Such a possibility was presaged by a breakaway group of the Nottinghamshire Miners' Association signing a district agreement with their coal owners and returning to work.

So the Federation called a conference. At it delegates showed they were against the Government's proposals by a four to three majority. Nevertheless they decided to recommend that the local representatives should open negotiations with their employers and report back. No agreements, however, were to be signed until a national conference could consider the reports. On 26 November they assessed the terms offered by the coal owners to the local repesentatives. In four cases the owners had refused to meet the miners' representatives, and in the rest the terms offered were derisory. However, that was the position and it had to be accepted. In despair the conference decided to abandon one of the Federation's principal tenets and leave it to the local negotiators to get the best terms from their employers that they could.

This was done, and by 30 November agreements had been concluded and work had been resumed in all the important coalfields. In the Forest of Dean it was not until 8 December that John Williams could meet the employers. They had said they would meet only him and a representative from each of the larger collieries chosen from men who were actually at work. This excluded all members of the union's Executive because none of them was working. John Williams pointed out that men in work were more likely to accept the owners' proposals than men who were still out. However, the owners would not modify their condition and John Williams went with a team of working miners to an all-day conference with the coal owners at the Speech House.

When they entered the room where the discussions were to take place, the atmosphere was frosty and the miners soon found they were up against

Food parcels being distributed at Bream towards the end of the strike. Many families would not have survived the lockout for as long as they did without aid such as this.

a stone wall. The owners said that the basis of any agreement must be the terms on which the men who had gone back were working, which included an eight-hour day, and that the agreement should last for five years. They said at first they were unwilling to discuss a shorter shift than eight hours, or the length the agreement should run for, or the reinstatement of the men still out. Eventually they conceded that the shift on Saturday should be of seven not eight hours and the agreement should be reviewed in three not five years. They were adamant, however, in their refusal to take back the men who had not yet returned to work, though they did grudgingly agree to look at individual cases. The men they had taken on, they said, were the ones they thought should have the jobs, and the men they would employ in the future would be the men they thought fit to employ. The good news was that they proposed a substantial increase in wages for December and January when the minimum wage would be 9s $10^3/_4$d per shift (about £17 in 1999). This, however, would drop each month thereafter until April when it would be 8s 3d, the same rate that had been paid for a seven hour day before the lockout.

John Williams was then asked brusquely if he was ready to sign the agreement. He asked for ten days to hold meetings of the men to get their agreement. They gave him a week.

He knew that 4,515 men out of the 6,500 men employed in April were actually back at work, with a further 487 on the colliery books waiting to be allocated jobs, and he realised that if the union agreed to the employers' terms, there was little chance of employment for the 1,500 men who had resisted returning. But he was also aware that the alternative to signing up to the owners' proposals was to have no agreement at all. In which case the men who had returned would have no security and in fact anarchy and endless trouble would ensue. He concluded that there was no alternative but to give in to the employers and sign.

On the following Sunday, a raw and foggy day, he called the men to a meeting at the Speech House. Only 450 of the 6,500 men concerned turned up. He told them the terms the employers offered. It was a dictated solution, he said. The men had to accept that 1,500 of them would not be taken back. He tried to console them by saying they were better off than in some other areas – in Durham, for example, it was estimated that 20,000 men would not be taken back – and, he continued, that was not the end of the story; there was still the possibility that those who had gone back might be put on part-time employment, two or three days a week in summer and four in winter, with of course a corresponding reduction in wages. He ended by paying a tribute to the men in the Forest who had remained loyal to the union and to their fellow working men to the end. They had been victimised, he said, and placed on the altar of sacrifice, as their fellows had been in every coalfield in England. With a despondent heart he advised acceptance of the employers' terms. There was practically no dissent and the meeting authorised him to sign the agreement.

Thus came to an end the saddest episode in the history of the Forest coalfield. After thirty-three weeks of strife and suffering none of the miners was a winner but those who lost most were the men who stayed out to the end. The men who had ceased to support their union and had decided enough was enough and returned to work, either early or late in the dispute, had come off best – at least they had got their jobs back.

Wage slip for Drybrook miner Charles Close for week ending 26 October 1926 after he had returned to work. Close was the buttyman of a gang of five, with whom he had to share the amount at the bottom.

88

EPILOGUE

The miners' defeat festered for thirteen years, until 1939, when coal for the war effort was needed and miners again became valuable workers deserving a decent level of existence. The thirteen years were dark ones, with much unemployment and short time. The failure of the general strike had tamed trade union militancy, and the lockout had broken the miners' spirit, removing any desire for further confrontation. But even though the lockout had ended in defeat for the miners, the experience was a warning to employers that it would be unwise to try to impose further wage cuts on them, even in small coalfields with high costs like the Forest of Dean.

After the struggle the coal owners remained linked nationally to the Mining Association of Great Britain, and they continued to insist that negotiations and agreements between them and their employees should be conducted each in their own coalfield. For ten years after the lockout there were no relations between them and the National Federation, to which the unions were affiliated. With two dozen different districts, all with their own agreements, the Federation was split into as many separate units. In some areas its effectiveness disappeared; in the rest its power was weakened.

In the Forest the number of miners employed fell considerably after the return to work. A fortnight after the dispute had ended there were 200 fewer miners at the New Fancy Colliery than before the stoppage and this was typical of the general situation. Numbers continued to fall until 1939. They never recovered their highest level post First World War level of 7,800 in 1920, or even the 5,000 of 1927.

Soon after the Forest collieries had settled down to the post-lockout world they began to close. The number of mines in operation dropped from 42 in 1927 to 31 in 1938. Not all closed because the coal they were mining had run out. Waterloo, it was estimated in 1946, had enough coal to last ten years, Cannop had enough for fifteen years, Eastern United for twenty-five, and Norchard and Princess Royal for over a hundred years each. Closures were caused in some collieries because it was becoming more difficult to mine the coal, in others because pumping out water was an ever-increasing problem. Whatever the reason the extra expense caused higher production costs and made it more difficult to compete against coal owners outside the Forest.

The Flour Mill Colliery ceased to wind coal in 1928. Crump Meadow closed in 1929 after 105 years service. Parkend Colliery also ceased to produce coal in 1929, though Parkend Royal pit operated as an emergency exit and Castlemain as a pumping station for the New Fancy. Foxes Bridge closed in 1930. Two collieries entered the war but did not survive it: Lightmoor, which closed in 1940 after serving for a hundred years, and the New Fancy, which closed in 1944 after producing coal for well over a hundred. Norchard finished in 1957, and Waterloo and Eastern United both closed in 1959. Cannop, which in the 1920s employed over 1,000 men and boys, went in 1960, a comparative youngster, only fifty-three years old. Princess Royal, which had been connected underground with Flour Mill and was the Forest's biggest colliery until it was superseded by Northern United, closed in 1962. Northern United was the last deep mine in Dean to go. No veteran of the lockout, it had been sunk in 1934 and closed at Christmas 1965.

Now all the big mines – and the smaller ones – have gone. Only a few free mines with one or two workers remain. The Forest of Dean Miners' Association disappeared when the Miners' Federation of Great Britain became the National Union of Mineworkers in 1945, and the devoted leadership given by its agents, H.W. Booth and John Williams, became legend. A last reminder of miners' trade unionism in the Forest can be seen in the Miners Welfare Hall in Cinderford, where the NUM banner is proudly displayed high on the wall.

Memories of the hardships of the general strike and lockout now remain only in the minds of a few old men and women, but stories of the struggle of those miners seventy years ago, of the men who wanted no more than enough wages to keep their families from hunger and bring up their sons and daughters in simple comfort, will never be forgotten.

APPENDIX 1

THE 1999 EQUIVALENT OF WAGES IN THE EARLY YEARS OF THE CENTURY

To say that in March 1921 a coal hewer earned 15s 3d (76p) a shift does not give the reader much idea whether he was well or poorly off, either in comparison with other workers at the time or with similar workers today. However, we can, by the help of cost of living or retail price indices, compare the cost of a basketful of goods bought by ordinary people in the 1900s with a corresponding basketful nowadays. One difficulty is that over the years the contents of the basket have changed considerably – people now buy television sets and pay for licences for them; they have refrigerators; and they no longer use candles and paraffin to light their houses!

Consequently new indices have been necessary periodically. To cover two widely separated periods of time these have to be amalgamated to make one smooth one, even though they are not related to one another and are made up of different components differently weighted. So we must accept that cost of living or retail price indices do not give a close comparison, though they can give a rough idea. Bearing in mind these difficulties, the use of a composite cost of living index (kindly produced by Lloyds Bank) shows that 15s 3d in 1921 can be said to be roughly equivalent to £20 in 1999. Other wages and amounts have similarly been translated and are noted in the text.

A further warning: prices and conditions of living have always varied over different parts of the country, and the consistently low level of the earnings of a Forest of Dean collier compared with his opposite number in, say, Yorkshire may not be so serious as it appears if food costs less in the Forest than in Yorkshire, and the Forester has more supplementary food supplies such as a pig in the sty and a big vegetable garden.

The severity of the cuts proposed by the employers (pages 33-34) is shown by the following Board of Trade figures. These take the average of the 1906-1910 cost of living index as 100:

1910	102
1914	106
1919	230
1920	266
1921	241
1925	186
1926	182

(Note: these figures support the 141% given by the Forest miner quoted on page 15)

NOTE: 1s (one shilling) now equals 5p. There were twelve pence (12d) in a shilling and twenty shillings (20s) in a pound (£1).

8. LIGHT MOOR COLLIERY

Lightmoor Colliery from the north, about 1910. The waste heaps in the centre foreground eventually became the tip which remains as a landmark to the mine to this day. The nearer engine house still stands, albeit minus its roof and is in an extreme state of neglect. It housed a 40inch Cornish pumping engine which has survived and is now restored to working order at the Dean Heritage Centre at Soudley. Note the reservoir provided to keep the mine engines supplied with water.

APPENDIX 2

DIARY OF THE GREAT STRIKE
WHICH COMMENCED APRIL 1ST 1921
by
W. D. MEREDITH
Manager of Lightmoor Colliery

On Thursday the 31st of March 1921 I was requested by the craftsmen's representatives to attend a meeting of that body in the blacksmith's shop with a view to obtaining promises that necessary pumpmen would remain at work. I reluctantly did this, and pointed out to about 60 who were present the serious position this colliery would be in, and also the district, if such a mad step was taken as to allow the pumps to stand even for six hours.

Mr Bernard Edwards after considerable discussion proposed, and it was unanimously carried, that the necessary pumpmen should remain at work. Not being satisfied even with this I put it to those pumpmen which were present "Did they intend personally to adhere to the decision arrived at" – the answer being in the affirmative. Mr. K. Trotter, under manager, and myself purposely to be in readiness in the event of the above arrangements failing, drew up two schemes –

> *1st. Allowing for certain sections to stop away*
> *2nd. Allowing for all stopping away*

That same evening, viz. 31st March, a meeting was held of the craftsmen at Cinderford, at which it was decided that no safety men should be allowed to go to work, with the exception of the necessary men to get horses out of the pit by the following Monday.

On April 1st Mr Trotter and myself arrived at the colliery at 5 am, and not knowing what had transpired at Cinderford the previous evening we were astonished to find all the craftsmen had withdrawn their services with the exception of those few men mentioned above who came to assist in raising the horses and the inspectors who are in a separate organisation and had personally assured me they would stick to me – come what may – and kept their promise.

Naturally this placed us in a very precarious position, and scheme No. 2 (previously mentioned) was put into operation. We detailed overmen, inspectors, also certain clerks and officials to go to the various pumps which were naturally unattended, and to do the best they could under the circumstances, and although this was attended with various mishaps and caused us great anxiety for the moment, they acquitted themselves with great credit. Having overcome this difficulty our next step was to make final preparations for the TOTAL withdrawal, which was threatened for 10 pm the following night (Monday).

Mr Trotter undertook to be responsible for the large Cameron pump at the bottom of the Big Pit. Mr R. Morse, one of the overmen, with three inspectors undertook to see to the feeding of the boilers underground, and I should like to here at once say how gratified I am for the energy they put into it, and for the long and strenuous hours they worked without a murmur.

Having raised the horses by Monday evening, to our great discomfort and inconvenience the remainder of the safety men at 10 o'clock that evening left us without men or fireboys for the Cornish pumping engines. Mr Addis, engineer, and myself had to take on these duties, doing both firing and attending to the engines. The first 5 days we worked continuously with only 6 hours rest, but as time went on we were gradually eased. We trained others to relieve us, Mr. H. Dix, and Mr. Wm. James, and eventually by training Mr. C. Francis, we filled up this department. At the shaft bottom Mr. Trotter attended to the bottom pump.

On the Friday during the first week we had a most alarming experience. Our Cornish engine, being a condensing engine, suddenly gave notice of failure due to an accident to the air bucket, which meant withdrawing the bucket – a very big contract – and we were much concerned as to whether we should be able to overcome the difficulty with the limited number of hands at our disposal. But come what might, the few of us left (about 6 where usually about 12 are employed on this job) decided to tackle the job, and after a laborious all night's work we overcame the difficulty, although at one time it was thought the colliery would be lost. Tremendous difficulty was experienced in withdrawing the air bucket. We found that the piston rings were broken in hundreds of pieces, and the great mystery is that greater damage did not occur.

Our regular pumpmen were at colliery to receive their last pay and saw the very awkward position we were in, and apparently sympathised with us. They wished me to order them to come to work. I replied I would do nothing of the sort. They could see how Mr Addis and myself were situated, and if they would not come voluntary I should not press them, but would rather take the whole responsibility of the whole colliery going under.

They then asked if they should see Mr Allen, the craftsmen's agent, and ask his permission, stating that if they did not come the colliery and the district would be lost, to which I told them to "please themselves". I understand this was done, which drew the remark from that gentleman "Let it go under". They therefore did not turn up, leaving us to face the situation best we may.

Owing to the Cornish pump being a condensing engine, having to stand so long, we took the risk and sent for Mr. Wm. Mountjoy, who is used to working our duplicate engine at the middle of the shaft, which deals with the water which otherwise would have flown down the pit and drowned the colliery. Although he was strictly forbidden to come to work he turned up and worked these engines, and I may say, although coming quite secretly, he has rendered us great assistance up to date.

On the following day we had another alarming accident. Our feed-water ramrod on the same engine buckled, but with perseverance we overcame this trouble. This with minor accidents underground finished the first week which was most exciting and busy for us all.

On April 11th we had another set back which gave us cause for anxiety. Our Mr Trotter met with a bad accident which might have turned fatal but fortunately only put him out of action for a few days. A joint which was under pressure of 220 lbs per square inch blew. Although running great risk, he stuck to his post and stopped the engine when the column of water settled back, hurling him across the pit bottom. We had then to arrange to train two more to take charge – Mr. Bert Probyn, checkman, and Mr. Ted Buffry from the office staff.

As the strike proceeded, the working getting better organised somewhat relieved the pressure upon us. By arranging the office staff to unload coal and attend boilers on surface, by the end of the fourth week instead of Mr. Addis and myself being at the colliery the greater portion of the 24 hours, we were able to have something like normal rest.

In passing I may say both the Miners' Federation and the Craftsmen insisted upon the withdrawal of the winding engine men. This was another big obstacle to be overcome, and nothing was left for it but to take this duty upon myself, although it was an awful responsibility, and one which greatly perturbed me. The engineman who lives on the ground kindly volunteered to be in the engine house whenever necessity arose for the raising and lowering of men, and I may say that as the days passed I gradually gave the engine over to him, staying with him as camouflage.

Mr Davis stayed away for a few days, and then came up to the colliery some time each day claiming that he was entitled to work as a shareholder, and as the excitement of the strike somewhat subsided he continued regularly.

Being so fully occupied at Lightmoor Colliery I had overlooked the question of Speech House Hill Colliery, and 12 days after the commencement of the strike I with Mr. Addis paid a visit to this place, which, of course, was quite idle and all fires out.

On the 14th of May we found that our Lightmoor holds at the bottom of the pit had become completely filled with water. We did not work the pump at the bottom of the pit during the night. This filled me with consternation and I immediately came to the conclusion there was something abnormal happening. It brought to my mind that the pumps at Speculation pit had not been worked for some days at the commencement of the strike, and that the water which had accumulated at that colliery must have found its way through to the bottom of the Speech House Pit from where it gravitated to the bottom of Lightmoor Pit.

I rushed over to Speech House, travelling the Cannop Level to the bottom of the Speech House Pit, and found that this was the case. I then organised a pumping shift to deal with this water at the Speech House between the hours of 12 and 6 each day, thus relieving the pressure of work at the Lightmoor Colliery. I also instituted a night pumping shift at the bottom of Lightmoor Colliery, and this combination has put us in very comfortable circumstances up to date.

Up to the time of writing, I cannot say how I appreciate everyone's effort in what they have done to safeguard the Lightmoor property. With the few hands for such a large colliery I should have not have thought it was possible, but not one has considered time or convenience, and it is only by these means that the colliery and district has been saved. Addis, Dix and myself from April 5th to April 25th were on the colliery for 354 hours, or an average spread over that period of 17 hours per day, and all of us have turned our hands to anything which was necessary, irrespective of position. I must especially mention Mr. Trotter, under manager, Mr. Addis, engineer, and Mr. Dix.

Speech House Hill Colliery circa 1910, after it had closed for coal production but was still in use for pumping Lightmoor. The site is now a car park and picnic area.

APPENDIX 3

SAVE THE MINERS AND SAVE ENGLAND
By M.P. Price
(Published in the *Gloucester Strike Bulletin* on 8 May 1926)

This crisis has been ripening for a long time. Back last summer it very nearly came, but was only put off by the appointment of the Coal Commission. This was the stop-gap to enable the Government to organise strike-breaking bodies all over the country. But they have failed.

The coal industry of Britain is sick. The reasons for this are:

(1) Revolutionary discoveries in applied science, such as

    (a)   use of oil in ships

    (b)   use of new types of boilers, economising fuel

    (c)   use of water power abroad for generating electricity, thereby dispensing with exported English coal

    (d)   development during the late war of coal-mining in countries which formerly imported only from England.

(2) Wasteful methods by which private capital, invested in coal-mining, carries on its operations; as for instance

    (a)   paying dividends during the war equal to the whole of the capital value of the mines in 1914

    (b)   issuing large amounts of capital which represents no real value, but on which the industry has to pay interest.

The result of all this is that:

(1) there is more coal produced in this country than can find a market

(2) the coal-owners are faced with the problem of having to earn large profits in order to pay interest on capital which is often borrowed.

As a result of (i), there is cut-throat international competition. The German coal-owners cut the wages of their miners in order to undersell British coal in Hamburg. The British coal-owners reply by getting the British Government to grant a subsidy to their industry, and this goes to cheapen the export price of coal and results in British coal being quoted cheaper than German coal in Hamburg. Now the German Government threatens to grant a subsidy to the German mines, if the British subsidy does not stop.

In France the situation is not much better, and the French coal-owners, in order to save themselves from a crisis in their coal export trade, are compelled to refuse German coal, which they ordered Germany to send them some years ago under the provisions of the Versailles Treaties.

Thus the national and the international situations react on one another. Each country tries to beggar its neighbour and, in the hunt to get rid of the surplus coal and sell it at prices which will undercut the prices of French and German coal, the coal-owners in this country bleed either the taxpayers, in the form of a subsidy, or the miners, in the form of wages, beaten down to the starvation level. This anarchy cannot go on. It must be stopped at once, and that is what the organised workers of England, under the auspices of the Trade Union Congress, are trying to do.

Two measures can be undertaken to save the situation:

(i) The mines can be brought under the control of a single organisation. This organisation may at first have private capital, i.e. private capital under State control, as a preliminary to nationalisation. This will have the effect of causing all the superfluous and inefficient mines, which are no longer needed, owing to the general world slump in coal, to be closed down. The nation will then be left with those mines that are the best and most efficient and have the most modern machinery. The Government must then make provision out of the taxes for the support of those miners who lose their occupation as a result of this inevitable change. This would mean that the coal subsidy should continue, but not as it has been paid in the last nine months, whereby mine-owners who were already making profits were entitled to draw, and did draw, the subsidy. The subsidy should only be continued in order to enable the miners who have lost their employment to tide over the difficult times.

(ii) Steps must immediately be taken to enter into an international agreement between all the great coal-producing countries of Europe, *viz* Britain, France and Germany, with a view to limiting the amount of coal which each of these three countries turns out each year and with a view to deciding in which of the foreign markets this coal shall be sold. Arrangements of this kind on an international scale have already been come to in regard to potash and incandescent lamps, and can also be come to over coal, because the coal industries of France and Germany are suffering from the same causes as ours is.

It is to stop the rot that the Trade Union Congress has decided to use all the industrial forces at its command to compel the coal-owners to face the situation. *This is not a strike against the community. It is a strike for the community.* If the Trade Union Congress is beaten the British coal industry cannot be saved. It will go down in chaos and disorder and starvation will face millions of workers in this country.

Public control of the coal resources and an international agreement can alone save the country. The coal-owners and a large section of the capitalist class of Britain are trying to ruin the miners – the miners who toil in the bowels of the earth in the midst of heat and dust, with danger dogging their footsteps every minute of their lives. It is for this reason that the Trade Union Congress has cried, "*All hands on deck! Save the miners! Save the country from capitalistic anarchy! Save England from a breakdown of her great and vital industries! Help Europe to a brighter future, of which England is a great and indispensable part.*"

APPENDIX 4
COLLIERIES IN THE FOREST OF DEAN 1926/1927

Name of Colliery	Owner	Employees underground	Employees overground
Arles Level Short Standing, Coleford	Gwilliam Bros	7	2
Arthur & Edward (Waterloo), Lydbrook	Lydney & Crump Meadow Collieries Co Ltd	600	80
Bridewell & Mailscot Gale Christchurch, Coleford	Gwilliams & Hawkins	8	4
Brominghold Berry Hill, Coleford	Parton Collieries Ltd	closed	
Cannop	The Cannop Coal Co	720	200
Cross Ash Berry Hill, Coleford	W.G. Nelmes & Sons	5	7
Crown Parkend	Parkend Deep Navigation Collieries Ltd	incl. in New Fancy total	
Crump Meadow Cinderford	Lydney & Crump Meadow Collieries Co Ltd	400	100
Dark Hill No 3, Ellwood	Darkhill No 3 Colliery Co	10	4
Drybrook Farm	A. Preest	?	?
Eastern United, Ruspidge	Henry Crawshay & Co Ltd	538	83
Farmers Folly Short Standing	J.H. Gwilliam	6	3
Foxes Bridge Cinderford	Foxes Bridge Colliery Co Ltd	579	123
Harrow Hill, Drybrook	Wigpool Coal & Iron Co Ltd	68	15
Highmeadow, Coleford	S.G. Hughes	10	3
Hillersland, Coleford	G. and E. Hughes	7	3
Hopewell Drift Edge End, Coleford	Hamblin, Milson & Sons	5	3

Hopewell in Wimberry Wimberry Valley	Bixlade Colliery Co Ltd	14	5
Hopewell in Wimberry Cannop	G.H. Jones	6	3
Howbeach, Parkend	Howbeach Collieries Ltd	102	63
Lightmoor & Speech House Main Cinderford	Henry Crawshay & Co Ltd	761	206
Lower Dark Hill Fetter Hill, Coleford	Rudge Bros	4	1
Mapleford Bixlade, Coleford	Gwilliam Bros	closed	
Marion's Vale Berry Hill, Coleford	Adams Bros	6	3
Milkwall Gorsty Knoll, Coleford	Lydney District Collieries Ltd	9	1
New Fancy Parkend (including Crown and Parkend Royal)	Parkend Deep Navigation Collieries Ltd	c520	c140
New Hawkins No 1 Level Bakers Hill, Coleford	A.W. Brown	8	22
New Regulator, Cinderford	Taylor &Roberts	18	11
New Speedwell Berry Hill, Coleford	Bayham, Frank & Brown	5	2
Nine Wells Five Acres, Coleford	Nine Wells Colliery Co Ltd	18	5
Norchard, Lydney	Park Colliery Co Ltd	400	70
Oldcroft, Lydney	The Oldcroft Collieries Ltd	100	25
Park Hill Colliery	Wilda Collieries Co Ltd	closed	
Parkend Royal	Parkend Deep Navigation Colliery Co	incl. in New Fancy total	
Pastor's Hill Colliery	Wilda Collieries Co Ltd	closed	
Patches & Lonk Level Christchurch	Hughes & King	9	3

Pluck Penny Moseley Green	Pluckpenny Colliery Ltd	closed	
Princess Royal Bream	Princess Royal Colliery Co Ltd	1,000	186
Prosper Gale, Coalway	Smith Bros	9	2
Reading Horne Hillersland, Coleford	M. & O. Gwilliam	9	3
Shutcastle, Bream	Thomas Peglar	20	13
Steam Mills Cinderford	Lydney & Crump Meadow Collieries Co Ltd	–	9
Thatch Edge End, Coleford	Edward Hughes	7	2
Trafalgar, Drybrook	Henry Crawshay & Co Ltd	closed	
Upper Dark Hill Fetter Hill, Coleford	F.R. Pardow & P.J. Perkins	6	3
Valletts No 1 Level Howlers Slade, Coleford	A.W. Brown	7	4
Weavers Pitching No 2 Bream	Wilda Collieries Co Ltd	closed	
Well Level Berry Hill, Coleford	E. Parritt & Co	closed	
Well Level No 2, Berry Hill, Coleford	E. Parritt & Co	closed	
Winnell Fetter Hill, Coleford	Brown & Ellis	6	3
Worcester No 2, Coleford	G.W. Morgan	3	2
Worrall Hill, Lydbrook	J. Wheatstone	5	4
TOTALS – Underground – Overground		6023	1403
TOTAL NUMBER EMPLOYED			7426

Note: The total number of employees shown would include managers, clerks, engineers and others not classified as miners.

When details were obtained nine of the 52 collieries were closed; in two cases the figures were combined with a third; and in one case no figures were given. The number of men employed were:

Number employed	Number of collieries
Under 10	13
10 - 19	11
20 - 99	5
100 - 499	3
500 - 699	4
700 - 799	1
800 - 899	–
900 - 999	2
Over 1000	1
	40

The information in this Appendix was taken from *The Colliery Year Book and Coal Trades Directory 1927* from details supplied by Forest of Dean colliery owners. It is unlikely to include every colliery in the Forest; nor perhaps was every listed colliery owner a member of the Colliery Owners' Association, which body organised the 1926 lockout. It is therefore not possible to say how many mines on the list were affected by the lockout.

Harrow Hill Colliery, near Drybrook, features in the centre of this mid 1930s view. At the time of the strike 83 men were employed here, 68 of whom worked underground. Note the size of the spoil tips which even a small mine such as this could produce.

APPENDIX 5

MARCHING TO THE WORKHOUSE
by Idris Roberts

I have never spent Christmas Day in the workhouse. But I did one day have a snowl of bread and cheese and a cup of cocoa in the workhouse.

It was on August 27 1926. I remember the date because on our way to the workhouse I saw a *Daily Express* poster opposite the church in Blakeney which announced '**Valentino Dead**'. And anyway it was 1926 because it was the year of the General Strike, and it was because of the strike I had bread and cheese in the workhouse. It happened this way . . .

I was sitting on the green opposite our house (I still live in the same house, and the green is still there, and back in this August I gathered a hatful of mushrooms for breakfast). But that August in 1926 I was a boy of thirteen, on holiday from school and gathering a boy's daydreams, when there came straggling up the hill from Pillowell a long line of men, their coats thrown over their shoulders in the hot August sun.

They were coalminers. My dad was among them. They were the men of West Dean, marching to Westbury workhouse to join the men from East Dean. It was a hunger march, and truly one, for the men from East Dean were going to ask for food from the workhouse.

The General Strike had ended long ago. It lasted less than a fortnight. Beaten by Baldwin, the railwaymen and the others gave in and left the miners in the lurch. The miners buckled their belts and carried on. It was hard; how hard two instances I personally recall will illustrate.

I was asked to go up to Tom Price's, the village shop, for two ounces (not a packet, not a quarter but two ounces) of tea. Old Tom weighed it, put it in one of those tricorn sweetpackets, screwed it up to stop any wasting, and gave it to me. It was 'on tick'.

The other occasion was when Mum sent me round to Mrs. Jones next door to borrow half a loaf of bread. Not a loaf, but half a loaf, mark you; it was when I discovered the truth of the old saying that half a loaf is better than none.

But out of those dark days fun sometimes shone. At least it was fun to my boyish bravado. Many of the miners dug their own coal during the strike, some simple outcrops, some miniature pits (one of them was so successful he didn't go back to the mines but set up as a coal merchant).

Me, I became a wicked capitalist coal owner. On the side of the tunnel at Moseley Green I dug me a level, like the one at the Norchard, only smaller. It went in at least four feet, and I put up some props, and almost every day that summer holiday I carried home a bag of my own coal.

And the day I am telling you about, in August, 1926, was fun too, at the time, although now I look back I can realise its stark tragedy. As the men went by the green one of them called out to me and said; '*Come and join us*'. So I joined them, and became their mascot on the thirteen-mile march.

Every so often we would sit down and rest. But one older man – Reub Elliott, I think it was – never sat down. Each time we marched he fell behind until he was the tail-ender. But when we sat down he marched past us, his coat over his shoulder, and gave us the 1926 equivalent of a Harvey Smith!

At Broadoak, one of our sitting places, some boy, one of the Harrises, found a hen's nest and gave me two eggs. As we passed an orchard a farmer invited us in to have as many plums as we wanted.

About three miles before Westbury a man walked to the front and made a speech. They said he was a Communist, whatever that was, and came from Cardiff. He must have been because he said; '*Good luck. I'm going to go back now, because the police will be waiting for me at Westbury.*' At the time, I remember, I thought he was a bit of a coward.

At Westbury we all sat on the bank opposite the workhouse and sang *Jesu, Lover of My Soul* to the tune of Aberystwyth. Then we were invited into the workhouse and given a snowl of bread and cheese and a cup of cocoa. I didn't ask for more.

(This account of one of the marches appeared in the *Forest Review Annual 1983* and is reproduced by kind permission of the *Forest of Dean & Wye Valley Review*.)

APPENDIX 6

FORESTERS' VIEWS
ON STRIKES AND LOCKOUTS
IN DEAN

When I was a boy of 13 I went down the pit to work at Lightmoor. The following year in March 1912 there was a strike by all the miners in England for a daily minimum wage. You would go into the pit to work but if you made a day's wage or what you thought was a day's wage, you would not get any more; the boss would not pay it out. And that was prevalent all through the country; you only had what you earned. Very often a man would be in a very hard place, awful difficult to make a living. So they all came out on strike. They were out a month and they won it. Every miner no matter who he was, when he went down the pit he was always sure he'd get his money made up if he could not get it. That was the first time the minimum wage was paid out in the country, in March 1912.

Harry Barton

I remember in 1912, I think it was, when the chaps were on strike they used to play marbles in the street. There was nothing much about.

Anon

[In 1921] the unemployed miners soon got to work digging over the dirt mounts for small coal. One area turned over was at the edge of a wood by Crump Meadow field, the Monkey Wood, and it was here where a heap of ground about a hundred and fifty foot square, three foot high, covered with grass, was dug over for the coal contained in it. It must have been part of the Crump Meadow dirt mount and the proportion of coal to dirt was good. It was an offence against company rules to send up even small quantities of dirt with the coal, so if a shovel contained only a handful of dirt and the rest of it coal it would either be thrown into the gob or brought out to be tipped. Consequently the dirt mounts contained a good proportion of coal. The men with picks and shovels turned over the dirt and picked up each individual lump of coal by hand to fill the sacks to be taken away in wheelbarrows or by horse and cart. Young as I was [seven years old] I had my sack and was picking coal for my mother when I was recognised by two of my uncles who had a large amount of coal for bagging up. They put an amount of about twenty or twenty-five pounds in my bag, lifted it onto my back and pointed in the direction of home. The weight was too much for me and I had to rest; unable to get the bag on my back again I dragged it in easy stages and eventually got it home.

Harry Roberts

Crump Meadow colliery pictured prior to the First World War, at a time when production and employment was at its height. Note the incorrect spelling of the colliery's name on this commercial picture postcard – 'Medow' instead of Meadow!

I can't tell you much about the 1921 strike – I was only about seven then – but I do remember once playing with older children watching for blacklegs going to work at Waterloo. We hid in the bracken and when we saw them we slipped away and told the men on strike in the village. They hurried off to meet the blacklegs and shout abuse at them.

Winifred Foley

It's called Waterloo but its real name is Arthur and Edward. Two brothers, belonging to the coal owner, come into the colliery and their names were Arthur and Edward. But the men didn't like the idea because they were not very fond of the coal owner. So they put their own name: Waterloo. I don't know if it was anything to do with the Battle of Waterloo or whether there was plenty of water down there or what, but that's what they called it, and it stuck and is called that to this day.

Harry Toomer
(Author's note: the Battle of Waterloo was in 1815; the colliery was opened in the 1840s. It was probably named after the nearby Waterloo Mill.)

I remember very well the children during the 1921 strike having to go to Five Acres School to have their dinners, which was soup.

Ted Gwilliam

I can only remember one strike, and that was when my mother was alive. She shouted something and the police on horseback pushed her back and she fell on her side. She went and had her leg off.

Mrs. L. Harmer

I can remember as a small boy going with my father down to Knockley Wood where a well known representative of the miners, Mr Ben Tillett, was going to address the miners. He hailed from the north-east and the period was during the 1921 strike, and he predicted that the road ahead for the miners would be difficult. How right he was. Five years later came the 1926 stoppage. When work did resume it was two and three shifts per week. This continued until a year or so before the outbreak of the Second World War.

You remember the evacuation of children from London and the home counties in 1939-40? Well, there was another evacuation of children from the Forest in 1926. They were miners' children from large and medium families. Every family in our area was at that time given a meal ticket from the Board of Guardians at Monmouth. There wasn't any cash or state handouts as we know it today. Every family with four or more children was asked to let a child go to foster parents in London and district. My sister Phyllis begged Mum and Dad to let her go. It was either that or your meal ticket for four children would be reduced to three. The children from our village of Bream were taken down to Whitecroft Railway Station and sent by train to Paddington.

On arrival each child had a label tied to their coat with their name and address on. Each child was placed on a pedestal and viewed up and down. Then came a shout from one of the organisers: 'Who wants this child?' My sister was very lucky being fostered by a Lewisham police sergeant and his wife, and they still thought of her as their daughter until the day they died. I believe some children settled in with their new families and never came back to the Forest.

I can remember when the mounted police arrived in Bream from Cheltenham during the strike to escort the miners in the Friar's Level and another pit at Clements End Green to and from work. Words were hurled at them for daring to go to work, but never the intimidation we saw on television in the miners strike in 1984. The strike was far from over for the wives and mothers of miners on the resumption of work. Families had had food on the slate, and this was being paid for years after the strike ended.

Hylton Miles

In the 1926 strike I was one of the children who were evacuated from the Forest and sent to stay with people in London. They were mostly working-class people who sympathised with the strikers. I was about twelve, thin and gawky, and Mam dressed me in the best clothes she could find. But that wasn't much. I had a thin dress, a darned cardigan, black boots that were too tight and a brown velvet hat which originally had a wide brim but someone had cut most of it off.

When we got to Paddington Station all us children were put in a sort of cattle pen in front of a lot of people who took us away, one by one. Soon there were only two of us left, me and a thin, round shouldered, girl called Florence. Then there was only me. No-one wanted me and I hung my head in shame. As I was wiping away my tears, a kind young man came up to me and said he would take me to a house in Kent. But first he took me to an office – I think it might have been Transport House – where the typists came to look at me and tease me. The man came back and told them off.

Then we set out for Plumstead in Kent. On the way we went to the restaurant on the station. He had a cup of tea, and ordered a ham sandwich, a bun and an apple for me. I ate the apple, core and all. I even ate the stem, as I didn't want to dirty the plate. When we got to Plumstead and the young man knocked at the door, the woman said they had ordered a boy, because of the accommodation. But when she saw how hangdog I looked and how disappointed the nice young man was, she said 'You may as well stay. We'll manage somehow.' But it was a very kind family and I stopped with them five months before I came back to the Forest.

Winifred Foley

During the strike mounted Metropolitan Police were stationed at Lydney and in view of the possible violence or misdemeanour they formed a posse and patrolled Whitecroft, Parkend, Fetter Hill and Coleford and returned via Sling and Bream to Lydney.

Cyril Elsmore

When he was on strike in 1926 dad was with a group of men down at Ranters Green. Percy Moore, the managing director of the Princess Royal Colliery came down the road. He ran the windscreen down and shouted out to our dad, 'When you coming back to work, Jesse?' Our dad said 'When you pay us a living wage, Mr Moore.' He said, 'I'll see you all eat bloody grass first!'

During the strike the children had a cooked meal every day at school, seven days a week. You took your knife and fork and plate under your arm. Burdess the underground manager of the Princess Royal Colliery who was on the Board of Guardians wanted, along with some others, to cut it, so the children would have only four cooked dinners and three bully beef sandwiches. Of course, our dad, Albert Brookes and Oliver Hoare opposed it. They said they believed that growing children should have a cooked meal every day, and fought hard and they won this. When those three went back after the strike they were walking back across the top of the pit. Burdess saw them coming. He said, 'There's no work for you three. You can bugger off.'

Hylton Miles

Three blokes in Bream put a fuse they had, gelignite, under Burdess's house. They fused all under there (of course, they were experienced miners who were

108

blasting rock). They would have blown that house to Kingdom Come with him in it. After they had lit the fuse, they all went their separate ways, in the early hours of the morning. Trouble was his wife and children were in it. That was what this one thought of, the one that went back. He thought 'Oh this yunt right,' and went back and put a wet turf over it and put it out.

Anon

I got cause to remember the 1926 strike. I was joint secretary of the union in Cinderford and I had 17 months victimisation for that. Jesse Hodges – you've heard of Jesse Hodges – and me were joint secretaries. They kept us out for 17 months. And do you know – truth is stranger than fiction – when I went to work for the Ministry of Labour I signed both managers on that had victimised me for 17 months!

I didn't have a very good time in the strike. I was married and we managed somehow. We got through and we never had any help from anywhere. And we never went without a meal. We had good neighbours – old Bill Wilkins, we were mates. He had a big garden and what he'd got I could have 'cos we didn't have a big garden.

Albert Meek

In the 1921 strike the horses were brought up to the surface at Crump Meadow Colliery and turned out to graze into what was known as Crump Meadow Field, while the horses from Lightmoor grazed in the White Hart Fields. A horse got away from the field by the New Fancy and ran all the way in a mad gallop to a ditch in the Green by what was the Dog Inn in Victoria Street where it fell sideways and got wedged and unable to get up. A small crowd gathered including children, and the pig-killer was sent for and in a short time he arrived with a humane killer and we all saw the struggling animal die.

Harry Roberts

I can recall another lad and myself sitting on the trunk of a tree and watching the men bring the horses up out of the mine at the Flour Mill at the commencement of the 1926 strike. The squeals of the horses on seeing sunlight for the first time was a sight I shall never forget.

Hylton Miles

It was very rare a horse was treated badly, always well cared for, and men got attached to their own particular horse. They took the horses out of the pit during a strike when they knew it was likely to be a long one. I don't suppose they liked going back in very well.

Harry Toomer

They didn't bring the horses up regular. They did only come out in the strike. They used to put a piece of sacking over 'em, look, to stop the direct light. They was wandering about for days. They didn't know where to go or what to do. They couldn't see, look. They did just stand and stare around, they had been in the dark so long.

Alfred Warren

They didn't pull the horses out when they shut the mines, mind. They was shot down there.

Eric Warren

In the big strike of 1926 I was working with my brother Jack at Crump Meadow and he decided to go back because we hadn't got nothing and it was hard times, mind, though we wasn't starving. Our Jack decided to go back and kept asking I to go back and I said 'No, I ben't a-coming. I shan't go back. I be a Labour man and I be on strike and I'll go when it's settled.' Well, we wasn't pushed as hard as some, but I'm not saying it wasn't hard, because it was. But it wasn't too hard on we, because we could go and have fruit. We used to go off with the farmer, shooting all down around Flaxley, and come back with a dozen rabbits and him would chuck me a couple. Well, that was something to take home, wasn't it? And we had a good, big garden. We got plenty of spuds and green stuff and mother used to bake her own bread.

Alfred Warren

[At Elwood] the biggest tragedy in our school life was the 1926 miners' strike. Most of the working population were miners employed at the various pits in the district. Some safety men continued working to maintain the conditions in the pits. The few exceptions who were not miners were Forestry Commission employees.

It quickly became apparent that children needed food. Our headmaster, Mr Joseph Pope, called a meeting of parents. The response was very good. They formed themselves into working parties and the Chapel schoolroom was taken over. Among the main stalwarts were Elijah Sayce who was responsible for the room and lighting the fire and cooking, and Charlie Fletcher who was brought up in Muller Orphanage in Bristol and came to Marsh Lane to learn the trade of mining. He did all the menial jobs. He always brought Mrs Thorne's dog, who usually lay on the grass in the cemetery, but one day he wandered around and someone stumbled over him carrying hot water and scalded his back. Charlie took off his coat and wrapped the dog up and took him back to his cottage. He looked after him and because his back was bare of any hair Mrs Thorne knitted several jerseys for the dog to wear until he was well.

On school days the senior children were designated to help. The main job for the boys was fetching firewood from the Forest, but we also needed coal. In this we were very fortunate for there was a very big coal-tip quite near the school, We brought small picks and filled buckets with the small lumps of coal salvaged from the tip. We were supervised and issued with the following instructions: 'All girls picking coal must stay at the bottom, whilst boys must go to the top of the tip.'

Also the boys fetched the water for cooking purposes from a spring at the back of the school in Marsh Lane. Each boy had a yoke and two buckets. Having filled the buckets we had to place bracken fronds on top of the water to prevent any spillage. I still possess the yoke my father provided for me.

The food was obtained from various sources. The headmaster was allowed a grant from the Relieving Officer to purchase essentials such as bread, cheese, margarine or lard. This was delivered by Mr John Jordan who had a small shop on the Milkwall Road. He had a box-type sidecar attached to a BSA motorcycle which he used to start with a handle under the saddle. If the machine was out of order, the boys used to collect the food in wheelbarrows.

The farmer, Mr T. Hoare, provided potatoes, swedes and skimmed milk. To compensate him when it was harvest time all pupils' fathers readily gave their help to gather it in. Other vegetables and fruit were brought by the pupils themselves from their gardens. When it was time to eat, we all marched down from the schools to the Chapel with a knife, fork and spoon. To avoid confusion in serving Mr Pope devised a system of tickets: white for potatoes, green for cabbage or other vegetables, and once a week we had red tickets for meat.

We sat down at table with newspaper tablecloths, mostly the *Forest Guardian*. When finished, we each washed our own plates and cutlery in a bath of hot water outside. This system continued until the end of the strike. This was truly a magnificent effort by a small community to feed the children.

Cyril Elsmore

A general view of Steam Mills about 1910 – a desolate looking spot! Many miners lived here and the village was hard hit by the strike. Even today, families recall men paying off debts incurred with local shopkeepers some 2 to 3 years after it had finished.

At Bream the children's meals were provided at school, each child took his knife, fork and plate for lunch. The meals were cooked by the female members of the Bream Labour Party and the waiting on was carried out by the male members of the Party.

Hylton Miles

The conditions we had to put up with were terrible. I went to school and we sat in the class and we had no food in the house. We marched from Steam Mills School to Bethel Chapel for the only meal we had in the day, and that was soup. And coming home we sat out on the bank by my home and saw the mounted police escorting the blacklegs home, and they'd come up around and more or less harass you. I'll never forget that – how could I? My father was a miner, my brother was a miner, and they used to go in the woods and chop wood or loll about on the banks – it was about all they could do. They used to shout at the blacklegs, that was why they had the police to escort them.

Jack Pritchard

Not many went to work during the strike but there were some. Out of necessity, you know, because nobody had got anything. They were all in the same way, some stuck it out, but others had to go back to get a shilling. My late brother Horace, he'd been off work for such a long time and eventually he went back. Then them on strike would come around and if they knew you were going back they would come outside your home and batter pans and tins and make a hell of a row. No fighting or anything like that, you know. And I can remember a couple of occasions the mounted police came down and watched my brother and a few more in Soudley into Eastern and back.

Alan Drew

I was at Lightmoor in 1926. I had saved some money by then. I was saving up to get married. Then that knocked it on the head for a time. But I'll tell you what we did – what was being done (I didn't do it). It was more than for fun. Just above the Dilke Hospital there used to be an old colliery, Woorgreen they called it. Now, I got to find out they were digging for coal up there when the strike was on, and selling this coal. One of my friends, a chap called Sid Cooksey (he married my cousin Lil Young) asked me one day if I'd go up with him. I said 'What for?' He said to get some coal so he could sell it for his home. 'Look,' I said. 'I don't want the money. I've been all right.' But he was a married man, so I said 'I'll go.' So we took another man called Stan Rogers up with us. (He was a relation, he married a cousin of mine.) We went up there and searched around and there was sure to be a hundred miners up there digging holes to get the coal out. We looked around, and well, we thought, they had all got the best of the plots, we got no chance at all. There was a siding there where they used to run the heavy wagons. There was the rails still there. I went across on my own and started scraping down between the sleepers and I hit the coal – 18 inches of coal.

It was all the way up the railway line. Other blokes had been digging their hearts out and they didn't know that. I called my mates over quietly and said 'Let's rip this all across there.' We got three and a half tons of coal out from there in about five hours. We sold it to Westbury Union (the Workhouse) for £3 10s.

Harry Barton

The old colliers was digging around various places, down at the furnaces and getting nubbles of coal, probably as big as a pop alley, you know. There was lots and lots of coal, buckets and bags of it that was found which was flung out as ash originally.

Alan Drew

One of the places where miners got coal was just off the road almost opposite the Fancy. There was a four foot seam of coal there only eight feet down, They'd dig a square, twelve foot by twelve foot, chuck the dirt out of the way, and there they'd have four foot of coal. They'd get that out and go in three foot on all four sides under the dirt. By only going in three foot they didn't need to timber-up. One man ignored the rule and went in further and got killed. Then they'd start the whole process over again six feet away and chuck the dirt in the first hole, and then on again filling the previous hole. I was only twelve then and still at school. Lew Lewis, he was at school with me, but he was eighteen months older and he went there to help his father and brother. He was at it for six months and never went back to school. The coal had to be guarded at night. Lew, who was on guard at one time, was found fast asleep leaning against a tree trunk next morning. A consortium of lorry drivers bought and collected the coal and paid £2 per ton, twice the pithead price.

Harry Roberts

As a lad I went up to Wet Wood off the Cannop Road with my father where he and his mates were digging coal in a strike pit. It was only a shallow seam and they went down a ladder to get the coal out. They worked night and day. The coal was taken off by the Gwynn family in a horse and cart. This started them off on their haulage business.

Hylton Miles

I remember my father [Fred Warren] dug coal in the strike pits with his mates. I was five at the time. They did it at night in secret so the pickets and the police did not know, and they slept nearby in the woods in the daytime. They dug at Mallard's Pike and elsewhere. They cut a four to five foot hole and went down a short distance, making a sort of bell pit like the old miners used to, starting in one corner and getting the coal out and then moving on, filling the corner with dirt. They went underground in a level and propped up the roof. I remember my father cutting off the root of a tree and using it as a pit prop. Rossiter & James of Parkend came to the site with a lorry and loaded the coal on it and paid

High Street, Cinderford, quite possibly at the time of the strike; many miners are gathered in the street. Also shown is the Town Hall, left, where many miners' meetings were held.

the men. But they were convinced in the end by the union that they were blacklegging and gave it up.

Eric Warren

In 1926 there were some of these strike pits. There was one at Steam Mills. Oh dear, there were two brothers sorting out timber from a stack for a pit. They flung over the stack and there was a boy sitting the other side and some timber flung over killed him.

Gilbert Roberts

My mother and I, our family were turned out of our home because we couldn't pay the rent. How can one forget that? We went to Westbury. I spent several days in Westbury Workhouse. And to have to endure that! There was no food, there was nothing. We had to rely on what was given to us by voluntary bodies. I can well remember a load of fish coming from Russia and being distributed around Ruardean Hill. I can remember it although I was too young to understand what it was all about or what was happening, But to think – we had fish delivered from Russia! It came up on the railway and my father was one of those who had to dish it out to locals so that they had something to eat.

Jack Pritchard

I remember my father going up the steps of Cinderford Town Hall to get a pound of sugar and a bit of margarine. I don't know who was giving it out.

Eric Warren

My father was out of work from 7 May 1926 to 11 November 1926 and he never had as much as a penny from anywhere.

Eric Morris

I was up here in the Forest during the strike. I was in Waterloo. We didn't have no union money but we did have summat from Russia, so they did say. 'Bout three or four shillings they did send and that had to last a month. I did run into debt – I ain't ashamed to say it – up at the shop at Woodside. I had all the food I wanted and I think I owed him 'bout £40, but I paid him, mind. His name was Willy White. He was good enough to let me have the things and I paid him back.

John Gwynne Griffiths

I was only five at the time of the 1926 strike but I remember the the Triangle and Station Street in Cinderford were choc-a-bloc full of people and police. I was standing by the railings of Bilson School and saw a man with his wife stagger past with his head all bleeding. He had been hit with a police baton.

Eric Warren

I was about twelve during the 1926 general strike. I lived in Cinderford, where practically every man was a collier, and bicycled to Coleford every day to work in my father's butcher's shop there. My job was to deliver meat to customers and I remember taking it to the 'Feathers' and the Police Station where they billeted the mounted police that had been brought into the Forest. They were brought in in case of rioting, because the colliers were very militant. In fact there was no rioting, only a little skirmishing at pit-heads.

People in the Forest were very poor in those days, and many would have suffered more during the strike if they didn't have a pig in the sty, grow vegetables in their gardens and run sheep in the Forest and did some swapping. In my father's butcher's shop they took the vouchers the union issued. Mr Griffiths was in charge of the vouchers. I don't think the union redeemed them all afterwards – they just didn't have the money.

Lionel Voyce

My father was the man who set up the union, brought the *Daily Herald* into the Forest, gave his life blood for the workers. He fought all the way. He was a moderate man; he wasn't violent. He could meet the bosses, he could meet them on their own ground. But he never believed in strikes. He would say to the men, 'Let me arbitrate and I can do better for us than striking, because [if we strike] there is nothing for us but the workhouse bread.'

I have left too much of my blood in the mines to ever want to go back down and I would not wish it on anybody. It was a pity it was ever discovered. I don't believe God meant for a man to grovel in the bowels of the earth and to leave blood on coal.

Jesse Hodges

Some of the above recollections were given to the author direct, others were taken with permission from tapes held by the Dean Heritage Centre, Soudley, and from *Forest Voices* compiled by Humphrey Phelps. Two of Harry Roberts' contributions were taken, with permission, from his *Autobiography of a Forester* in the Gloucestershire Record Office.

BOOKS CONSULTED

V.L. Allen *Power in Trade Unions*
R. Page Arnot *The General Strike*
R. Page Arnot *The Miners. A History of the Miners' Federation*
 The Years of Struggle
John Burnett *A History of the Cost of Living*
Anthony Burton *The Miners*
G.D.H. Cole and Raymond Postgate *The Common People 1746-1946*
Cyril Hart *The Industrial History of Dean*
C.P. Hill *British Economic and Social History 1700-1982*
Keith Leybourn *A History of British Trade Unionism*
Keith Leybourn *Britain on the Breadline*
H.W. Paar *The Severn & Wye Railway*
J.A. Peck *The Miners' Strike in South Yorkshire*
Ian Pope, Bob How and Paul Karau *The Severn & Wye Railway Vol.s 1 and 2*
Ian Pope and Paul Karau *The Severn & Wye Railway Vol. 3*
Ian Pope and Paul Karau *The Forest of Dean Branch Vol 2*
Mark Stevens *Ernest Bevin*
Barry Supple *The History of the British Coal Industry Vol 4 1913-1946.*
 The Political Economy of Decline
Francis Williams *Magnificent Journey. The Rise of the Trade Unions*

ALSO CONSULTED

The Colliery Year Book and Coal Trades Directory 1927
The Forest of Dean Coalfield HMSO 1946
Transactions of Bristol and Gloucester Archaeological Society for 1972
Vol. XCI. Article by A.R. Williams *The General Strike in Gloucestershire*
*Dean Forest Mercury, Dean Forest Guardian, Lydney Observer, Gloucester Journal,
Gloucester Strike Bulletin*

ACKNOWLEDGEMENTS

My thanks go to all the people who have contributed to Appendix 5; to Hylton
Miles, Ian Pope, Pam Powell, Ruth Proctor Hirst, Roy Close, Roy Haviland,
and the Gloucestershire Record Office for lending me photographs; and to David
Bick, Nigel Costley, Averil Kear, Humphrey Phelps, Bill Punt, Keith Ray
(Manager of Lloyds Bank, Lydney), Tania Rose, Lionel Voyce, Elsie Olivey, the
Central Statistical Office, the Dean Heritage Museum Trust, the *Mercury*
Newspaper Office, Cinderford Library, the Gloucestershire Collection, the
Gloucestershire Record Office, Jackdaw Publications and *Punch*. Especial thanks
go to Neil Parkhouse for the use of material from the photographic collection of
The Archive Shop and for providing additional information for the captions.

INDEX

Adams Bros, 100
Addis, Mr, 94, 95, 96
Allen, Mr, 94
Amsterdam Trade Union International, 52
Archbishop of Canterbury, 52
Awre, 49

Baldwin, Stanley, 27, 29, 34, 36, 39, 50, 51, 54, 55, 56, 58, 63, 81, 103
Barton, Harry, 105, 113
Bayham, Frank & Brown, 100
Bevin, Ernest, 37, 56
Bixlade Colliery Co Ltd, 100
Black Friday, 21
Blacklegs, 58, 73, 74, 75, 77, 84, 106, 112, 115
Blakeney, 49
Bledisloe, Lord, 17, 62
Blewitt, W., 18
Board of Trade Statistics, 15, 30, 33, 91
Booth, H.W., 12, 16, 23, 90
Bowdler, Bert, *Frontispiece*, 19
Bream, 67, 107, 108, 112
British Broadcasting Corporation, 42, 52, 53, 56
British Gazette, The, 42, 47, 51, 52, 55
British Worker, The , 42, 46, 52, 53
Brookes, Albert, 108
Brown & Ellis, 101
Brown, A.W., 100, 101
Buffry, Ted, 95
Bullo Pill, 49
Burdess, T.W., 108
Bywater, Edwin, 42

Cannop Coal Co, 99
Cannop Foundry, 72
Cardinal Bourne, 53, 58
Cheltenham, 75, 76, 107
Churchill, Winston, 27, 42
Church of England Bishops, 81
Cinderford, 64, 72, 74, 75, 77, 80, 81, 93, 109, 114, 115, 116; Miners Welfare Hall, 90; Town Hall, 114, 115; Bilson School, 115
Cinderford Mercury, (*see Dean Forest Mercury*)
Citizen, The, 15
Close, Charles, 88
Coal Mines Act, 69
Coalfields: Bristol, 25, 84; Forest of Dean, *passim*; Kent, 25, 84; Lancashire, 25, 81; Somerset, 25, 27, 84; South Wales, 30, 81, 84; Yorkshire, 81
Coleford, 49, 108, 116
Collieries, pits and levels: Arles Level, 99; Athur & Edward (*see* Waterloo); Bridewell & Mailscot, 99; Broadoak, 104; Brominghold,

99; Cannop, 17, 22, 32, 71, 82, 89, 90, 96, 99; Castlemain, 90; Clements End Green, 107; Cross Ash, 99; Crown, 99, 100; Crump Meadow, 16, 60, 82, 90, 99, 105, 106, 109, 110; Dark Hill No. 3, 99; Drybrook Farm, 99; Eastern United, 16, 59, 71, 77, 82, 89, 90, 99; Farmers Folly, 99; Flour Mill, 62, 71, 82, 90, 109; Foxes Bridge, 16, 60, 63, 88, 90, 99; Fryer's Level, 73, 107; Harrow Hill, 99, 102; High Meadow, 99; Hillersland, 99; Hopewell, 72; Hopewell Drift, 73, 99; Hopewell in Wimberry, Cannop,100; Hopewell in Wimberry, Wimberry Valley, 100; Howbeach, 100; Lightmoor, 16, 18, 19, 33, 59, 60, 63, 70, 72, 77, 82, 92, 93, 96, 100, 105, 109, 112; Lower Dark Hill, 100; Mapleford, 100; Marion's Vale, 100; Milkwall, 100; New Fancy, 16, 61, 64, 71, 82, 90, 100, 109, 113; New Hawkins No. 1 Level, 100; New Regulator, 73, 82, 100; New Speedwell, 100; Nine Wells, 100; Norchard, 17, 62, 71, 82, 89, 90, 100, 104; Northern United, 60, 90; Oldcroft, 82, 100; Parkend, 90; Parkend Deep, 82; Parkend Royal, 61, 64, 90, 100; Park Hill, 100; Pastor's Hill, 100; Patches & Lonk Level, 100; Pluck Penny, 101; Princess Royal (Park Gutter), 20, 21, 24, 25, 62, 63, 71, 82, 89, 90, 100, 101, 108; Prosper, 101; Reading Horne, 101; Shutcastle, 101; Slope, 82; Speculation, 96; Speech House Hill, 72, 95, 96, 100; Steam Mills, 101; Thatch, 101; Thornton Reeks, 72, 73; Trafalgar, 12, 13, 60, 101; True Blue, 71, 75; Upper Dark Hill, 101; Valletts No. 1 Level, 101; Waterloo, 61, 82, 89, 90, 99, 106, 115; Weavers Pitching No. 2, 101; Well Level, 101; Well Level No. 2, 101; Winnell, 101; Woorgreen, 112; Worcester No. 2, 101; Worrall Hill, 101;
Colliery Year Book & Coal Trades Directory 1927, 102
Cook, Arthur J., 26, 27, 28, 34, 81, 84, 85
Cooksey, Sid, 112
Co-operative Societies: Forest Societies, 15, 23; Cinderford Society's store, 15; field, 77, 81
Cost of Living, (*see* Board of Trade Statistics)
Craftsmens representatives, 95
Cramp, C.T., 23
Crawshay, Henry, & Co Ltd, 60, 99, 100, 101

Daily Express, 44
Daily Herald, 17, 42, 116
Daily Mail, 36, 55
Daily Mirror, 42, 43